ONE

GOD

James A. Starnes

Order this book online at www.trafford.com
or email orders@trafford.com

Most Trafford titles are also available at major online book retailers.

Printed in Victoria, BC, Canada.

ISBN: 978-1-4251-9044-6

*Our mission is to efficiently provide the world's finest, most comprehensive book publishing
service, enabling every author to experience success. To find out how to publish your book, your
way, and have it available worldwide, visit us online at www.trafford.com*

Trafford rev. 3/15/10

www.trafford.com

North America & international
toll-free: 1 888 232 4444 (USA & Canada)
phone: 250 383 6864 ♦ fax: 812 355 4082

Dedication

This book is dedicated to the memory of my beloved friend, the Rev. Donald Joiner. Don did not agree with all of the content of this book, but he proofread it and offered me encouragement to publish it. We disagreed in love. Cannot the religious people of our earth do the same?

It was not what Rev. Joiner thought that endeared him to others, but that he was kind, and respectful, and helpful.

The Rev. Don Joiner personified the love that his Jesus preached.

About this book:

This book is for the serious reader who desires to use both head and heart to understand and appreciate the **'oneness'** we share with those of other faiths.

Rev. Starnes points out the strengths of the Major Religions of the World, presenting the basic beliefs of Judaism, Islam, Christian denominations, Buddhism and Humanism in a most entertaining, enlightening and thought provoking manner.

The dove of peace flies between the covers of this book as the author's theme of peaceful co-existence and peaceful co-operation calls us to be intentional and active peacemakers.

We hope everyone, whatever your religious preference, or even those who claim no religion, will read this book. It stresses the **'commonalities'** we share and the **'peace'** we all seek!

Comments from Tom and Molly Wilkes
(A clergy couple and dear friends)

ONE GOD

James A. Starnes

Preface

On September 11, 2001, the World Trade Center in New York City collapsed after an unprecedented and unbelievable terrorist attack. The terrorists commandeered commercial air craft and used them as suicide weapons containing thousands of gallons of combustible fuel. New York City, America, and the entire world shall never be the same.

Conversely, the communities of the world, the people of every nation; indeed, every individual who values life and prizes freedom, must do one's part to tear down walls of prejudice and hatred and violence. Simultaneously, we must each actively build bridges of better understanding and acceptance and tolerance of differences. Mutual respect is paramount.

This book of dreams is my attempt to help realize that greater dream of peace and harmonious relationships among us all. My dreams are imaginative encounters with people with different religious beliefs based on my previous experiences and research.

The objective of this writing: **to demonstrate that most religions have much in common; and in fact, more in common than at variance. I write toward the purpose that we can and must live in peace; or we will die in 'pieces'.**

Perhaps you would like to know a little more about the author's perspective. I am a United Methodist minister and a retired college professor. While behavior sciences are my area of expertise, I have taught major religions of the world courses at the collegiate level. I have also studied in a Buddhist temple, spoken in Jewish synagogues, and served as chaplain to Muslim inmates incarcerated in a state prison.

I still maintain a keen interest in religions; and have done extensive research. One other point that may be of interest to the reader: **I believe these dreams to be God sent.**

A PERSONAL NOTE FROM THE AUTHOR

After a sudden, shocking and very severe heart attack and by-pass surgery, I healed slowly. This near death experience and painful rehabilitation was an horrendous experience - involving depression, periods of religious doubt, and re-evaluation of my personal priorities.

During my healing process, I read profusely - the Bible, the Quran, books of sermons, biographies and autobiographies. Often, after researching a particular individual or a group, I dreamed of a conversational exchange with the subject of my research. These dream visits were usually in the form of an interview, with the dream visitor(s) telling me something of value.

After the dream, I almost always felt the compulsion to record it. I would rise and write out as much of the dream as I could remember. Since I am a retired United Methodist minister, an ex-college professor of behavioral sciences, and an ex-chaplain of a state prison system, many of the dreams are of a religious nature. In fact, I honestly believe these dreams to be divinely inspired. For the most part, they are about the people and principles of the books: the Old Testament, the New Testament, the Quran, and advocates thereof.

However, if you choose to believe that these dreams are not divinely inspired, simply evaluate them as my best thoughts on various subjects presented in parabolic form.

An Introductory Dream

"Wake up, dreamer," the Voice demanded. "For God is calling."

On recognizing two women in my bedroom (fully clothed), I smiled, and then asked, "God in the form of two women?"

"Not exactly, but rather a God who speaks often to and sometimes through two women," one of the women announced.

Then the other spoke, "We know that you have read our book 'God Calling'."

"O yes, now I get it. You call yourselves the 'Two Listeners' and published your book anonymously back in the early 1900's and yes I have read it. It is beautifully written. You might be interested to know that I am recording some of my dreams also."

One of the two listeners responded, "That is why we are here tonight. To encourage you to keep recording your dreams. You are getting it down to the way God wants the book to be written. Stay alert; and keep recording, and when the time is right, God will cause the book to be published."

Getting back to their book, I asked, "As I recall, your divine messages were filled with thoughts of love, joy and laughter."

Listener one: "Yes, but conversely, our days were filled with pain, our nights tortured by chronic insomnia, and poverty was our daily portion."

Listener two: "But still, with even God's face veiled to us at times and with fresh calamities coming upon us, came the insistent command to love and to laugh and to be joy-bringers to the lives we contacted."

"To laugh, to cheer others, to be always joyful amid pain-racked days… spare me that calling," I requested hopefully.

"But think of it," listener one suggested. "We are not in any way psychic or advanced in spiritual growth. Just very ordinary human beings, who have had more suffering and worry then the majority and who have known tragedy after tragedy."

Then listener two pointed out, "Your near death experiences and the visions you received after your surgery and painful re-covery have enabled you to also become a special listener to God's messages. Keep your pen and paper nearby, as we did. And listen…"

Then listener one concluded her visit, **"May love and joy and laughter fill the pages of your book** and the remaining days of your life… even if pain is your constant companion."

Listener two's final advice, **"May your book inspire your readers to respect different perspectives and to dream of peaceful cooperation among all religions."**

Together they concluded, "So let it be written; so let it be done."

Just after the year 2000,
In the year of the great prophet 1430,
and according to the Jewish calendar, 5770
I received some messages from God via dreams…
I felt God was willing me to record these dreams.

The following is what I remember:

My First Dream

An Islamic male, a devout believer of the Muslim faith, became convinced that it was Allah's will for him to take his own life. He had suffered much hardship because of his devoutness. He had also felt alone most of his adult life; and now a severe and continual ache throbbed in his head.

He sent for the mercy-killer, a female of the Christian faith who had a reputation for hastening the death of many in a painless manner. Instead of bringing him the death he thought he wanted, she brought life he had never known. It was mutual love at first sight. The elements of respect, empathy and kindness blended the relationship. The two became one; the Muslim male and the Judeo-Christian female. And they both knew it to be God's intended will.

After I had written down this first dream, the Voice spoke:

"This harmonious relationship among Jews and Christians and Muslims is My Holy will. For I am a God called by many names. I am a God sought by many religions and cults and God-seekers. I am the one God, the Creator-God, the Prime Mover, the Great Spirit, The Universal Cohesiveness. I say 'be' and it is done. I say 'no more' and your heart stops. I say heaven or hell; and you are judged. I say be as two lovers, respect each other's cultural roots and work together. I say this is My intended will and it must be so."

Then there was music, a multi-cultured choir singing:

"Hear O world, the Lord our God is **ONE**.
Hear O world, Yahweh's will be done!
Let us live together, as sisters and brothers;
As family, who honor our fathers and mothers.
As the people of the books...
As the people of the books...
Together forever..."

"Hear O world, the Lord our God is **ONE**.
Hear O world, Allah's will be done!
May God's peace, forever more increase;
Blended together in love and in peace.
As the people of the books...
As the people of the books...
Together forever..."

After the music, the Voice came again:

"Peace on earth and harmony among the peoples of the earth cannot be achieved as long as discrimination and prejudice and violence prevail. As long as any sister or any brother is victimized, then the system is not working."

The Voice got louder: "You must try harder, work longer, study more, speak out more effectively, dare to non-violently protest, and love your enemies more. Your religion must be expressed in loving acts of kindness. This is the will of your ONE GOD."

After I had received this dream and had awakened and recorded it in all the detail I could remember, I danced before God. As I swayed and waved my arms; my body rejoiced and expressed my worship. Then, in a spirit of peace and inspiration, I wrote:

"Peace on earth and harmony among the peoples of the earth cannot be obtained and perpetuated without the conviction and commitment and willingness of many of us to die for our cause. As long as one brother or one sister is denied, I am denied. As long as any sister or any brother is victimized, then the system is not working. We must try harder, work longer, study more, speak out more effectively, dare to non-violently protest, and love our enemies more. God help us to help ourselves. May we become the 'family' our Creator wills, blended together forever... in 'Agape' (**love**) and 'Shalom'(**peace**). Amen."

Table of Contents
(Abbreviated)

CHRISTIANITY

AND

JUDAISM

SOME EXCERPTS FROM THE OLD TESTAMENT

"In the beginning, **God**…" (Genesis 1:1)

"Then God spoke these words, 'I am the Lord your God, who brought you out of the land of Egypt, out of the house of slavery. You shall have no other gods before me.'(Exodus 20:1) This is commandment number one of the Ten Commandments.

The Shema: "Hear, O Israel, the Lord our God, the Lord is **ONE**." (Deuteronomy 6:4)

"Fools say in their hearts, there is no God!" (Psalm 14:1)

"And the Lord will become king over all the earth, on that day the Lord will be **ONE** and His name **ONE**." (Zechariah 14:9)

"What does the Lord, thy God, require of thee?
  …to do justly, to love mercy, and to walk humbly with thy God." Micah 6:8
  (This is the author's favorite Old Testament passage.)

"Or is God the God of the Jews only? Is he not the God of Gentiles also? Yes, of Gentiles also, since God is …**One**…" (Romans 3:29-30) Words of Paul, a devout Christian Jew.

A Recurring Dream

When I taught a class in Old Testament at our college, I invited the local Jewish Rabbi and a Baptist preacher to co-teach with me. The three of us created a more exciting learning environment, offering different perspectives, to say the least. For instance, I had prepared my course syllabus using a play on the word "history" which I called: "**His-story**, how God has acted in the Old Testament". However, Rabbi Kesner took issue with my referring to God in the third person pronoun. He suggested that we refer to God as **YHWH,** because Jews feel God's name is too holy to speak. Therefore, no vowels. When Jews see the word for God they pronounce Lord or Adonia. I decided to call my course: "YHWH, the God of the Old Testament".

To enhance the students' learning experience, the rabbi invited the class members to participate in a Jewish Seder at his synagogue. Since I am a proponent of John Dewey's concept of 'learn by doing', I happily approved this project.

My students prepared the meal according to the instructions given in the Old Testament, learned various parts of the ritual in Hebrew, and came to a different and impressive interpretation of this Jewish Passover feast.

As a result of this experiential learning, the death angel not only passed over our Passover ritual, but a ritual that had been 'dead' to my students, now became more meaningful to their lives. We also worshipped as a class at the Synagogue. When the guys put on the prayer caps, and the girls started at the back of the book of worship and read forward in Hebrew, most of he students came to a new appreciation of the Jewish people and in particular, of the Exodus from Egypt of an enslaved people. They now understand anew, the meaning of the First Great Declaration of Indipendence: Moses demanding, **"Let my people go!"**

Occasionally, I still dream of that Passover meal and of my students' reactions, and of those wonderful college days.

The Holy Land?

It was the closing moments of a very productive and peaceful day. I was sitting on the flat roof of a house in Israel looking into a western sky as God painted a glorious sunset over the Mediterranean Sea. I was chatting with Abuna Elias Chacour. He is one of the most Christ-like people I have ever known. This was indeed, a dream fulfillment.

Father Chacour told me of the Zionist soldier who had driven his family from their home and made them refugees in their own land in 1948. He told me stories of other horrible deceptions, then he invited me to take up the Palestinian cause; but only if I could do so with love in my heart for their violators and persecutors. He told me that because of Christ as his Lord, he could forgive and love the soldiers who had stolen his home. He told me that **God was not a Christian; nor was He a Muslim; nor was God a Jew. But that Jews and Muslims and Christians must become more God-like.** He affirmed that God loves all babies; and that God desires for us to play together, to share, to love each other as brothers and sisters in the land, for it is indeed meant to be a Holy Land for a holy people living together as sisters and brothers under the spiritual guidance of a Holy God.

I accepted his challenge and became a Christian counselor/ teacher, working in an interfaith school under the principalship of Father Elias Chacour, a Melkite Catholic priest who three times has been nominated for the Nobel Peace Prize. Father Chacour is also the recipient of the Niwan Peace Prize, which is bestowed by the Buddhist.

12

The remainder of this dream is about two of my students. She had just served a mandatory eighteen months in the Israeli army; he was the grandson of an Arab chieftain. They were both students in my human relations class. She, Jewish and he, Muslim.

I had assigned the students to 'empathize' with each other. She was to learn the five pillars of the Islamic faith and to read the Quran, from back to front. He was to participate in a Jewish Seder, read the Torah, and attend a synagogue worship service. Then they both were assigned to write essays on three of the following five Christian topics:

1) The Trinitarian concept of God
2) Jesus' concept of the Kingdom of God
3) The Parables of Jesus
4) The Miracles of Jesus
5) The life and letters of Paul

I wish I could tell you that both earned A's in the course, fell in love, married and became parents of three lovely children, one of whom grew up and became Jewish, another Muslim, and the third Christian; and of course, that they lived happily ever after.

Unfortunately, 'and they lived happily ever after' is more story book than reality. My dream became a nightmare when this Jewish girl discovered that her Muslim boyfriend was only dating her to learn of military defense strategies. She shot him as an Arab spy.

Even in the so called holy land we have three holy books: the Quran, the Old Testament, and the New Testament. All three describing the same Holy God. However, it seems to me there are too many holes and not enough wholeness in these three concepts of a holy God.

In order to live 'happily ever after' should we not all agree that we each have the right to disagree? My dream concluded with this reaffirmation of Voltaire's challenge: "Although I disapprove of what you say, I will defend to the death your right to say it".

My dreams are not for a synthesis of all religions; but rather, for a peaceful cooperation of all religions. Peace does not result in the total annihilation of all other religions; peace is the result of the family of humanity sitting down for a meal and enjoying each other's differences as well as commonalities. Then, rising together to go our separate ways, yet each working to achieve better relations among all peoples, even the unlovely and noncommitted. The dream theme was "Let there be peace on earth; and let it begin with us."

Father Chacour's closing advice was threefold:

1) **Love** your enemy; rather than trying to kill them.

2) **Forgive** rather than seeking revenge.

3) And **share**; without expecting anything in return.

Would to God we could all put hands and feet to Father Chacour's dream and join him in respecting the rights of others.

The Ten Commandments

After viewing Cecil Demilles' film, "The Ten Command-ments," Charlton Heston, who played Moses in the film, stood at the foot of my bed looking like he had stepped out of the screen... beautiful white beard, shining face, robe and sandals. However, in my dream, Moses cradled a rifle in his left arm.

"THOU SHALT NOT KILL," I called out.

"It is just for self defense," Heston responded. (You readers may recall that actor Charlton Heston was at one time the spokesperson for the National Rifleman's Association.)

"THOU SHALT NOT BEAR FALSE WITNESS," I called out again.

"Chill out," Heston's character, Moses, replied. Heston then motioned for me to follow him. We went outside and got into a new, baby blue Fleetline Cadallac convertible.

"THOU SHALT NOT MAKE UNTO THEE ANY GRAVEN IMAGES," I called out this time.

Heston then motioned for his three children to get in the back seat. He told me that he was taking the kids to be with his first wife. And of course, I called out: "THOU SHALT NOT COMMIT ADULTRY."

Just then one of the kids' portable phones rang. "It's grandma," the kid said, "and she wants to talk with you dad."

"God damn it," Heston said softly, "the old crow will talk forever."

This called for two commandments: "THOU SHALT NOT TAKE THE NAME OF THE LORD THY GOD IN VAIN;" and "HONOR THY FATHER AND THY MOTHER."

He told her he could not do that, that he had something more important to do. When he hung up, he said to me, "She invited me to go to church with her tomorrow." Then he said with me: "REMEMBER THE SABBATH DAY AND KEEP IT HOLY."

We both laughed as the children played among themselves. "Well, let's go for another one. Have you stolen anything lately?" I asked, expecting a resounding "No". Instead, actor Heston said, "Ironically, I actually stole the role of Moses from an actor friend."

"O no," I exclaimed. "Let's wrap up this dream. We have done every commandment except the first and the last. I am not going to ask you if you have broken them; rather, I request that you say them for me." I asked him to use his Moses voice.

He bellowed out most dramatically:

"THOU SHALT HAVE NO OTHER GODS BEFORE ME;" and "THOU SHALT NOT COVET."

Dreamer's note: "Moses is to the Old Testament what Jesus is to the New Testament. Besides these Ten Commandments, Moses also gave the Jewish people the Shema: **'Hear, O Israel, the Lord thy God is...ONE...'**"

8th Century B.C. Prophets

(from the Jewish Bible)

A conversation among Hosea, Amos, Micah and Isaiah...

Hosea: "Hey Amos, about what time do you think it is?"

Amos: "Well, I'd say it's about 750 b.c., give or take 50 years."

Hosea: "No man, I mean what time of day?"

Amos: "Oh, well it's still the first watch; I'd say it is a little past the 4th hour."

Micah: "Say, how do you determine that? You know, I never have learned to tell time. Someone needs to invent some type of thing we could wear around our neck or maybe on our arm."

Amos: "I just start at sun up and add the hours."

Micah: "Yeah, but what is an hour?"

Amos: "Each time the sand runs out of my hour glass I just turn it over and make a mark. Then I count the marks."

Micah: "And how about the year?"

Isaiah: "This will probably go down in history as the year that king Uzziah died; or at least, that is the way I am dating the scroll that describes my calling."

Micah: "Now that you have mentioned it, let me ask you something about your calling Isaiah. You said that you saw some seraphims, high and lifted up with six wings. What in the world is a seraphim anyway?"

Amos: "I'd like to know that myself. Is it something you city preachers have in your temple that me and Micah don't have out here in the country?"

Isaiah: "A seraphim is a winged celestial being of uncertain identity."

Micah: "Yeah, right. That's just more of that educated, city talk that means he doesn't know either, Amos."

Amos: "Course if the king is your uncle, you don't have to really know to get the first church in Jerusalem. Do you, Micah?"

Micah: "Well, like I've always said, 'It's not what you know; but WHO you know.'"

Hosea: "Now hold on fellows, let's maintain a good relationship here. After all, we are all working for the same cause: 'Trying to get these people to repent and come back to YAHWEH'S WAYS.'"

Isaiah: "Speaking of repentance, how is Mrs. Gomer doing these days, Hosea?"

Amos: "Yeah, or rather who is she doing? Ha, ha. Just kidding! Seriously though, we all hope she is still faithful."

Hosea: "I wish I could say she is still faithful, but she went back to the streets again. This time I bought her back off the slave market."

Amos: "Oh man! I'm really sorry man. I warned you not to take her back. One bad fig, you know."

Micah: "Yeah, he told you so."

Amos: "Haven't you learned anything?"

Hosea: "Look Amos, I just might take that plumb line of yours and wrap it around your neck if you don't back off. You guys just don't get it. I still love the woman. It's like God's undying love for us. What if Yahweh was to give up on us just because we sinned a little?"

Micah: "A little…"

Isaiah: "I still think Hosea is right to forgive her. And I do admire how he loves her. **His forgiveness is beautiful and reminds me of Yahweh's beautiful love for each of us. How great and wonderful and forgiving and compassionate our God is.**"

All the prophets said, "Amen!"

Hosea: "Say Isaiah, let's sing a verse of that song the seraphims sang at your calling. Start us off…

All the prophets sang together:

> "Holy, holy, holy, Lord God Almighty,
> Early in the morning, our song shall rise to Thee.
> Only Thou art holy, there is none beside Thee,
> God our Creator, **ONE for unity**."

Isaiah: "O.K. fellows, what are your final thoughts for the dreamer's readers?"

Amos: (preaching) "Woe unto you that desire the day of the Lord! To what end is it for you? The day of the Lord is darkness, and not light. As if a man did flee from a lion, and a bear met him; and he went into a house and leaned his hand on the wall, and a serpent bit him. Thus saith the Lord: 'I hate, I despise your feast days and I will not smell of your solemn assemblies. But **let judgment run down as waters, and righteousness as a mighty stream.**'"

Micah: (After the applause for Amos had subsided) "Same O, same O. What does the Lord Thy God require of you? **To do justly, love mercy, and walk humbly in Yahweh's ways.**"

Hosea: **"Dare to love, risk forgiveness,** trust and have faith in God and in people."

Isaiah: "Brothers and sisters, be humble and don't stumble and remember, '**great in our midst is the Holy One of Israel...**'"

And all the prophets said, "Amen".

ADAM and EVE?

During this dream. I am eaves dropping on a conversation between an ameba and a paramecium. They are unaware of my observation. **Note from the dreamer:** "In case you have forgotten your high school biology, an ameba (amoeba) and a paramecium are microscopic, single cell organisms. A reader will certainly need a good imagination to grasp the implications of this dream."

The ameba: "Hey Mecium, do you know where frogs come from?"

The paramecium: "Sure, from tadpoles. Why?"

A. "And butterflies?"

P. "From caterpillars." And again the paramecium asked, "Why?"

A. "Well, amphibians coming from fish; and beautiful butterflies from worms... all a part of what I started. I was the first, you know."

P. "Ha, you taking credit for all of creation. You are nothing but a spineless blob."

A. "Ouch, that was cold. But you make your point. After all, you did get the first digestive system and was the first to sexually reproduce."

P. "So, Ba, do you think these Adam and Eve believers will ever give it up?"

A. "You would think so Mecium, what with every high school kid dissecting worms and frogs. Surely they all know the instant completed man and woman is a legend; or at least a theory that cannot even answer the question: 'Where did Cain and Able find their wives?'"

A. "Still, they are not too far off when they say that God formed man from the dust of the earth."

P. "Yeah, but what difference does it really make whether they call you Adam and me Eve, or call a completed man and a completed woman Adam and Eve. We are all created by God."

A. "Amen Mecium, we are all God's creations."

P. "I guess it is the time factor that some of those completed ones cannot think beyond three dimensions. You would think that Einstein's theory would have taken them into the fourth dimension by now."

My clock awakened me!

"How appropriate," I thought. "Man's measurement of time versus God's."

Then I smiled: "How could a God have done it without man's invention of seconds and minutes and hours and days and months and years?" Then I thought, "A talking ameba and a talking paramecium. Boy, these dreams are really getting wild!"

from a Bitter Eve

...to a Better Eve

No one wanted to sit with her, but...

It was the only seat available on the bus; so I sat down beside her. She was very fat; with two big tits hanging down on her belly, and long grey hair hanging down her back. From the first, I smelled her body odor. In her hands she held two raw, oyster like gonadic looking balls.

"Christ," I exclaimed. "Are those symbolic of what they look like?"

"They sure are," she grinned. "Helps me meditate when I roll them around in my hands like this."

"You gotta be sick," I told her, as I flinched a little.

"Yeah," she agreed. "Sick of you bigot males screwing up everything and anything."

"Wait a minute," I instructed, "You have got no right calling me a bigot. You do not know me from Adam."

"Maybe not from Adam, but I sure as hell fire can distinguish you from Eve," the obviously anti-chauvinist stranger and strange one affirmed. "Let's take the Adam and Eve saga as a case in point," she continued. "Eve got blamed for Adam's weakness even in this very first, primitive story.

Why couldn't old Adam just have told God that he was curious and wanted more knowledge on the subject? Instead, he blamed Eve for tempting him. Typical of you men, blaming a woman."

"You make a good point," I conceded. "However, I am content to admit that both individuals in the relationship messed up God's nudist garden experiment. I am willing to see them leaving the Garden of Eden holding hands, having learned from their errors, and facing whatever their future of hard work may hold for them; still having enough spunk in them to raise a little Cain," I joked.

"I like that," she smiled, and for the first time I began to relax a little also. "Just maybe we can agree on some issues," I prayed within me.

"Let me add a thought," she broke in. "The most important concept in this Adam and Eve bit, and the main reason I am in your dream, is revealed by Eve in Genesis 4:1. For whatever your faith, and whatever your fate, it is with the help of God (whether a He or a She or a non-gendered Creator) that we are what we are."

I awaken from my dream with an attitude of gratitude, a lessened male chauvinist orientation; and, 'with the help of the Lord,' I took my pen in hand and recorded this dream.

The Patriarch?

"Father Abraham?" I asked the nocturnal visitor that had appeared in my bedroom.

"No," responded the nomadic dressed figure. "I am Abraham's nephew, Lot. I trust I have not disappointed you too much."

"Well, to tell you the truth, I have been reading extensively about your uncle. **Three great monotheistic religions trace their origins through Abraham.** However," I continued, "I do enjoy a lively dialogue; and from what I know of you, you seemed to have lived a pretty exciting life. This may prove to be a very interesting dream after all."

Lot: "So be it, but know that I was sent. Now, what would you like to know?"

Me: "Well, to liven this dream somewhat, let's start off with a little violence and sex. Tell me about that time when that mob surrounded your house wanting to rape those two strangers. How could you possibly offer that mob your daughters as surrogate sex objects?" (Genesis, Chapter 19:1-11)

Lot: "To understand that situation, you need to know how it was in that day and time; and particularly, to have been a citizen of the cities of Sodom and Gomorrah."

25

"Back then," Lot explained, "if a wife gave birth to a son it was a great blessing; conversely, the birth of a daughter was a great disappointment. Daughters were valued by the dowry their father's could arrange for their betrothal."

Lot: "Another accepted custom was the sanctity of guests within one's home. Even if the host family was poor, a fatted calf was roasted when entertaining guests."

Me: "You are saying that if I had lived in your day, or had been in your sandals, that I would have also offered my daughters to that mob. Not a chance."

Lot: "Then you are doing what so many people like you do. You are judging others by your value system and not by theirs. **One must study the historical setting, consider the mores of the original audience; try to understand the messages that the writer is attempting to convey to his unique audience in his time frame. Then, and only then, can one edify insightfully and relevantly.**"

Me: "Hey, that's heavy. I promise you I will re-evaluate my opinions based on what you have told me. But for now, let's go on to another topic. Lot, do you interpret the destruction of Sodom to mean that God condemns homosexuality?"

Lot: "No more so than the fact that God did not kill me when I impregnated both my daughters in drunken, incestuous affairs can be interpreted that God approves of incest. (Genesis 19:30-38) The real problem of Sodom was the unwillingness on the part of the men of that city to observe the law of hospitality which was the origin of the New Testament's golden rule (**Do onto others as you would have others do unto you**). And, of course, the wrongfulness of attempted gang rape!"

Lot summarizes: "Listen to me, both the good and the bad are printed in the Old Testament: natural catastrophes (like the volcano eruption that took out Sodom), wars and rumors of war, rich and poor, generous and greedy, love and lust, truth and lies. Just as Abraham chose to give a tenth to the priest, you too must decide about tithing. Abraham had unquestionable faith. You too must live with some degree of faith. I chose to live in a gay community. You too, in your time frame and point of reference, must deal with homosexuality. You must decide if your love is compassionate enough to include that different life style." (Genesis 14:17-20)

"Wow! This has really been a very interesting dream. Thank you for the thoughts you shared with me," I said to Lot.

"No need to thank me," Lot's image replied. "As I told you, I was sent. All that I have shared with you tonight are my thoughts. Now before I vanish, hear what my uncle wants me to emphasize to you about monotheism (**One God**):

'THOSE WHO CHOOSE TO WORSHIP THE ONE HOLY GOD, MUST ACCEPT ALL MEN AND WOMEN, WHO DO LIKEWISE, AS BROTHERS AND SISTERS. WE ARE ALL CHOSEN BY GOD TO LIVE IN HIS SPIRITUAL FAMILY AS SISTERS AND BROTHERS. ALTHOUGH OUR OPINIONS MAY DIFFER, THE DREAM IS TO LIVE IN PEACE!'

HOPE

I begin this dream as a Muslim, having just completed my pilgrimage to Mecca. I have circled the Kaaba seven times, reciting the parts of the Quran I know by memory. I was even permitted to kiss the Black Stone.

I have donated two and one half per cent ot my last year's gross earnings to an orphanage and since we are in Ramadan, I am keeping the fast obediently.

However, something is not quite complete. I do not feel as satisfied as I had hoped that I would. I feel similar to the results I felt after I had dream traveled to Russia, where I went below Red Square and saw the preserved body of Lenin.

And even though I dreamed as a black American, I felt that same void as I stood before the Lincoln Memorial in Washington, D.C., remembering the emancipation proclamation.

Then I dreamed of visiting Jerusalem. There I visited the traditional tourist sites. Finally I stood, and bowed, before the designated place of Jesus' burial, but the tomb was empty. I no longer felt incomplete and unsatisfied. I felt hope!

Then I remembered, "**Jesus was a Jew**"; and if I was going to better understand Jesus' way, then I needed to know more about Judaism. That Friday night I attended a synagogue service. I wore the prayer cap and started reading at the back of their book of worship forward.

A night later I dreamed I was in the synagogue where Jesus had read from the prophet, Isaiah. The host rabbi greeted me, "Welcome," he said. "There is a new dawn coming."

"Wonderful," I eagerly agreed. "But when? When will this new dawn come? When people can tell the difference between the sheep and the goats?"

"No," the rabbi smiled. "Nor when the people can tell the pomegranate tree from the olive tree."

"How about when the moon turns into blood," I quoted from the hymn.

The rabbi's answer: "No, the new dawn will come only **when people recognize the stranger as a brother or sister, and will treat them as family.**"

"Yes," I concurred; and then added: "The new dawn will come **when Christians and Jews recognize the enemy as a child of God and treat them as such.**"

As I was waking, the rabbi bid me goodbye. "Shalom," he said. "May your brokenness be made whole, healed and complete."

"Thank you," I replied; and returned his good wishes: **"Shalom to you and to all Jews. And may that peace that passes all understanding unite us as God's children."**

Post-test on Judaism

Please fill in the blanks (This is an open book exam. Have fun!)

1. **The Shema:** "Hear, O Israel, the Lord thy God is _____."
2. (Micah 6:8) **"What does the Lord require of you?**
   A. to do _____,   B. to love _____,
   C. to walk _____ **with thy God."**
3. "Jesus was a _____, and if (we) are going to better understand Jesus' way, then (we) need to know more about _____."
4. Father Chacour: "God is not a _____, nor is God a _____, nor is God a _____; but **Jews and Muslims and Christians** must become more _____."
5. Father Chacour, a Melkite Catholic priest, is the recipient of the Niwan Peace prize, which is bestowed by the _____."
6. The **dreamer-author's** dreams are not of a _____ of all religions, but for a peaceful _____ **of all religions.**
7. **Father Chacour's advice is: "**_____ your enemies rather than trying to _____ them, _____ rather than seeking _____, and _____, without expecting anything in return."
8. Isaiah: "I do admire how (Hosea) loves (his adulterous wife). His _____ is beautiful and reminds me of **Yahweh's beautiful** _____ **for each of us.** What a _____ and _____ God he is."
9. Lot: "One must study the _____ setting, consider the mores of the _____ (hearers), try to understand the messages that the writer is attempting to convey to his _____ audience in his _____ frame. Then, and only then can one _____ insightfully and _____."
10. How do Jews pronounce their word for God, **YHWH?**

CHRISTIANITY

AND

ISLAM

SOME EXCERPTS FROM THE QURAN

According to Mohammed, the angel Gabriel called Jews and Christians: 'the People of the Book'. In the Quran, 29:46, Gabriel recites: "And do not argue with People of the Book unless it is in a most kindly manner, except with those of them who have been unjust. Say (to them) 'We believe in revelation which has come down to us and in that which came down to you. **Our God and your God is ONE**, and it is unto God that we surrender ourselves.' "

About **LOVE,** a quote that may apply for relations between Americans and people of an Islamic nation: "It may be that God will grant love between you and those whom you hold as enemies. For God has power over all things, and God is Oft-Forgiving, Most Merciful." (Quran 60:7)

Quran 122: "Say, 'it is the **ONE GOD.** the Eternal, the independent cause of all being'."

"It is God, other than Whom there is no other god. Who knows all things hidden and open, who is the Merciful, the Compassionate. It is God, other than Whom there is no other god. The Sovereign, the Holy, the Source of Peace, the Guardian of Faith, the Preserver of Safety, the Exalted in Might, the Omnipotent, the Overwhelming. Glory to God, beyond any association they attribute. It is God, the Creator, the Originator, the Fashioner… to God belong the most beautiful names. Whatever is in the heavens and on earth celebrate God's praises and glory, Who is exalted in might, the wise." (Quran 59:22-29)

A Critique of Christianity by Mahatma Gandhi

This dream was stimulated by the movie "Gandhi". As my dream opens, the Mahatma, which means "great soul," is fasting because of the fighting between the Hindus of India and the Muslims of Pakistan. It is a peace fast.

A Hindu soldier comes before Gandhi's bed and begs his forgiveness and asks for his prayers. He confesses he has killed a little Pakistani boy to avenge his own son's death. Mahatma Gandhi offers him (and us) this advice:

"Go," he says, "and adopt a Muslim youth and raise him as your own son - except for one difference - although you remain Hindu, train your adopted son to grow up to be a believer in the Muslim faith. Teach him the best of the Islamic religion; and expect the best from him. You will find that Hindu and Muslim can live together as one family."

When E. Stanley Jones, one of my favorite Methodist preachers, asked Gandhi what he thought of "Christianity", he responded with four points:

"**First,** I would suggest that all of you Christians must begin to live more like Jesus Christ.
Secondly, practice your religion without toning it down.
Third, emphasize love and make it your working force, for love is central in Christianity.
Fourth, study the non-Christian religions more sympathetically to find the good that is within them."

"I believe the 'Great Soul' was right!" the dreamer, author.

My four comments about Gandhi's four points:

1) We Christians worship Jesus more than we follow him.

2) Most of us would never think of rejecting Christ, we just reduce His gospel.

3) Jesus Christ was love personified, and we must follow His example.

4) **Hindus and Muslims and Christians and Jews can live together as family - but in order to do this, we must respect each other and expect the best from each other.**

* Note from the dreamer/author: "If you have not seen the movie: 'Gandhi', I highly recommend it's viewing."

Barefooted before the Maker

This dream began with me on my knees in a mosque. I was kneeling with about fifty other men, all facing the same direction, and we all had our shoes off.

I had my shoes off because everybody else had taken theirs off. They had taken theirs off because Moses took his off at the burning bush. Moses took his off because God told him he was on holy ground. The point being: where we were praying was considered to be holy ground.

Everyone was praying out loud, the same thing, but in a foreign language.* While I did not recognize this language or understand the prayers, I felt the worshipers were sincere. I knew that I was; and I believe God realized I was sincerely worshipping.

As I leaned forward, following the example of everyone else, and placed my forehead on the floor, I prayed, sincerely:

> "O Lord God, Creator of the universe,
>   Whom the Jews worship as Yahweh,
>   and the Muslims as Allah,
>   and the Christians as trinity,
>   **Hallowed be thy Holy NameS."**

* Since I was very curious as to what my fellow Muslims worshippers had prayed in Arabic, the next day I researched their prayer ritual. The following is a translation of that prayer:

34

(However, one misses the soothing sound of this prayer when recited orally with others in Arabic.)

"In the name of the Merciful, Compassionate God...

Praise be to God, Lord of the worlds, the Merciful, the Compassionate. King of Judgment day. You alone we worship; and You alone we seek help from. Guide us along the right path: the path of those You have blessed; and not those upon whom is Wrath, nor the Lost. Amen."

* Note from the dreamer/author:

" This beautiful prayer is the opening chapter of the Quran. Muslims believe that the same archangel, Gabriel, who spoke to Mary, the mother of Jesus, 'recited' the Quran to Mohammed over a thirty three year period."

A Baptist Preacher
And An Islamic Imam

After reading several surats from the Quran, I went to sleep praying that I, too, might receive a dream vision from the angel Gabriel. Instead, I dreamed of a conversational exchange with our local Imam; a personal friend.

"Jerry, if you would permit me, I would like to be perfectly honest with you about my doubts," I begged.

"Before I was a Muslim Imam, I was a Baptist preacher. I understand an inquiring mind," he laughingly replied. "Please feel free to be completely honest; as I will try to be with my answers."

Needless to say, he surprised me by his response. "Well," I said, "I am shocked. You had not told me about your previous ministry. I just assumed that you grew up as a Muslim. From Baptist clergyman to Imam is quite a change. Why did you switch?" I asked.

He began: "One major reason was the color thing. Back then, Christianity was mostly a white man's religion. The Islamic faith offered a better career choice for a man of color."

He continued: "I also felt, at least in the Baptist denomination, that we were becoming more and more a Jesus cult. Jesus worship turned me off; and I believe would turn Jesus off also. Your Christ pointed to his heavenly Father, not to himself. The emphasis should be upon Allah (Praise His Holy Name); not one of his prophets.

"Then you denounced the divinity of Christ," I interrupted.

"That is true," he agreed. "I tried for years to honestly believe in a Trinitarian concept of God; but I met so many narrow minded protestants who insisted that Jesus was the only way. To me, Jesus was an outstanding prophet whose emphasis was on expressing **a compassionate love for one's neighbor based on the grace of a forgiving God.**"

My Imam friend concluded: "I believe that Allah (PHHN) intended for Jesus to live and to teach to a ripe old age. His death was incidental, not central. God's will was no more for Jesus to be killed then His will is for war, or for a child to die accidentally. Therefore, the importance of the teachings of Jesus must be evaluated in the light of the post-resurrection, Pauline doctrine. In short, Jesus is not the problem, Paul's teachings about the Christ is... and those who preach Paul's Christology rather than **Jesus' parabolic teachings of love and justice.**"

Then my Muslim friend added: "One other constructive criticism if I may, you Christians stress the individual too much and the community of believers too little."

I admitted, "You certainly have given me some food for thought. But now let me share with you some of my doubts about the Muslim faith."

He nodded, and I began: "The angel Gabriel gave the Quran to a man who could not even write? Especially some of the beautiful Arabic verses contained in the Quran? And why was

Mohammed the last of the prophets? Could Gabriel not recite again through another man or woman?"

He flinched when I suggested Allah (PHHN) might speak through a woman. I took the clue: "And the way most male Muslims I have met treat women is unacceptable to my sense of fairness. Remember that your founder married a rich, forty year old when he was just twenty five; and that it was her money and support that enhanced his ministry. I feel certain he treated Khadijah fairly. Besides, I have read the Quran through twice, from back to front, and I recall the surat: 'The pursuit of knowledge is obligatory over every Muslim, male or female.' **If your fundamentalists can read...**" I let the sentence fade out to accentuate the point.

Then I continued: "I also have questions about the history of the black stone and also about the Muslim interpretation of Abraham's sons. And one more, some of the things that Mohammed credit's Jesus are not found in the New Testament - like that 'flying clay birds' bit."

"I see you are well read," my Imam vision complimented me. "Can we agree that the holy books of both Christianity and Islamic religions contain poetic language? But that both the Bible and the Quran encourage a high standard of living, teachings of brotherhood, belief in one God (assuming that the trinity is a concept of one God), and that belief in and submission to the holy will of this one God, whether called Allah or Yahweh or Almighty God, is the ultimate commitment? After all, I have discovered that **the closer we get to the Creator- Creating God, the more likely we are to get closer to each other.** Do you agree?" he asked.

"Of course I agree," I joyfully responded, "but is that enough? Can we live together on this earth in peace? You must remember that both religions contain 'Great Commissions': the call to win the world in the name of their religion. Do you think we can change these thoughts of world-wide conquest to world-wide cooperation?"

The Muslim Imam: "To me, peace does not mean total annihilation of all opposition. I advocate peaceful co-existence. However, **if the fundamentalists of either religion prevail...**" He let the sentence fade to make his point.

As my dream began to fade, and as I awakened, I heard him say, "Record this dream accurately, for it contains an element of hope. However, if we cannot live peacefully and cooperatively on this earth, I think it unlikely we could co-exist peacefully in a heaven somewhere. If the spirits of Abraham and Jesus and Mohammed are still alive, surely they live harmoniously."

Excerpts from a speech by Barack Obama
(Addressed to the Muslim world from Egypt)
The Year 2009

esident Obama:

ssalaamu alaykum. (Applause) I'm a Christian, but my father me from a Kenyan family that includes generations of uslims. As a boy, I spent several years in Indonesia and ard the call of the azaan at the break of dawn and at the fall dusk. As a young man, I worked in Chicago communities here many found dignity and peace in their Muslim faith.

s a student of history, I also know civilization's debt to Islam. was Islam -- that carried the light of learning through so any centuries, paving the way for Europe's Renaissance and lightenment. It was innovation in Muslim communities that veloped the order of algebra; our magnetic compass and ols of navigation: our mastery of pens and printing; our derstanding of how disease spreads and how it can be healed. amic culture has given us majestic arches and soaring spires; neless poetry and cherished music; elegant calligraphy and aces of peaceful contemplation. And throughout history, am has demonstrated through words and deeds the ssibilities of religious tolerance and racial equality. pplause)

also know that Islam has always been a part of America's ory. Since our founding, American Muslims have enriched the nited States. They have fought in our wars, they have served our government, they have stood for civil rights, they have rted businesses, they have taught at our universities, they've celled in our sports arenas, they've won Nobel Prizes, built r tallest building, and lit the Olympic torch. And when the first Muslim American was recently elected to Congress, he took the oath to defend our Constitution using the same Holy Koran that one of our Founding Fathers--Thomas Jefferson-- kept in his personal library. (Applause)

So let there be no doubt: Islam is a part of America. And I believe that America holds within her the truth that regardless of race, religion, or station in life all of us share common aspirations--to live in peace and security; to get an education and to work with dignity; to love our families, our communities, and our God. These things we share. This is the hope of **all** humanity.

All of us share this world for but a brief moment in time. The question is whether we spend that time focused on what pushes us apart, or whether we commit ourselves to an effort--a sustained effort--to find common ground, to focus on the future we seek for our children. And to respect the dignity of **all** human beings.

It is easier to start wars than to end them. It's easier to blame others than to look inward. It's easier to see what is different about someone than to find the things we share. But we should choose the right path, not just the easy path. There's one rule that lies at the heart of every religion--**that we do unto others as we would have them do unto us.** (Applause) This truth transcends nations and peoples--a belief that isn't new; that isn't black or white or brown; that isn't Christian or Muslim or Jew. It's a belief that pulsed in the cradle of civilization, and that still beats in the hearts of billions around the world. The people of the world can live together in peace.

Thank you and may God's peace be upon you." (Applause)

Blue Eyed Blondes and

Black Skinned Africans

Again the One said to me during a dream: "Receive and record so that they may have hope: 'Behold, a black male traveled in southern U.S. of A. in the days of racial unrest. His automobile malfunctioned and he found himself alone on a desolate stretch of road in the rural south.

Three white men, drinking and looking for excitement, happened by. They stopped to help; but decided instead, to rob the stranger, and to beat him and to smash his car.

After the three left, the stranger stood there - beaten and robbed - grateful to be alive, yet angry that he had been violated and ashamed that he had not tried to over power his attackers. He worried about what would happen to him now with no money and no transportation.

Suddenly and surprisingly, a second car approached. Four people were in this car - two blacks and two whites, two men and two women. The black male was coupled with a white female; a white male was coupled with a black female. The white female was a Christian believer; her black friend was a Muslim. The black female was a non-affiliated seeker; and her white friend was Jewish. They offered the stranger a ride; and a new hope. (Remember: this unlikely event is a dream!)

Note from the dreamer: "There need not be prejudice (prejudgment), nor violence, nor hatred. Jesus' parable about the good Samaritan tells us how to live as neighbors. Malcolm X discovered it on his trip to Mecca: 'There were tens of thousands of pilgrims from all over the world. They were of all colors, from blue-eyed blondes to black-skinned Africans, but all were participating in the same ritual, displaying **a spirit of unity and brotherhood.'**

Brother Malcolm failed to include 'Sisterhood'. In the dream parable I was given, **women are equal and/or superior."**

An Afghanistan Woman

"Hello," I said to the bundle of clothing that stood before me. "Anyone under there?" I asked.

Only silence was returned to my question.

Again I addressed the completely covered figure: "Hello, is anybody home?"

Again, only silence.

"Look," I addressed the figure for the third and probably the last time, "This is just a dream, a figment of my imagination, my unconsciousness. No one can hold you responsible for what you say; so why not talk with me. I would like to know what an Islamic woman thinks about some of today's problems."

Still silence; but to my surprise, she removed her veil. "Hey, I know you," I said. "You are that news broadcaster I saw on television last night. You are Afghanistan's Voice of Radio. How nice of you to appear in my dream. Thank you for this blessing."

"You seem to be a kind man," she began. "But you are a man. And as our Quran teaches, Adam was created first; then Eve was created for Adam's pleasure. Therefore, Islamic women are taught to be submissive to men."

44

My rebuttal: "Dr. Evelyn Laycock, a dear friend and by far the best teacher I have ever studied under, tells that same creation story a little differently. She declares that after God had created Adam, He said to Himself: "I CAN DO BETTER THAN THIS." Then He created woman and said, "Now, this is very good.""

My Afghanistan visitor smiled and responded: "Nice interpretation; but it is obvious your friend does not live in a Muslim run country."

"Your point is well taken," I complimented her. "And I can only imagine how tactful and cautious you must have to be in expressing yourself in your country. But in other countries, gender is not an issue; nor color; nor class. What is an issue is the educational level of a nation's people. **Ignorant people with a religion are still ignorant people,** I concluded.

"Yes," she concurred. "**It is going to take both religion and education!**"

And with that powerful statement, she replaced her veil and disappeared.

9 - 11, 2001

The night of September 11, 2001, I just could not forget the sight of that second plane flying into and totally destroying the World Trade Center. The horror caught on film was more like a science fiction movie than reality. How could anyone do such a dastardly deed? And to do so in the name of religion? Unbelievable.

Finally, I dozed off, still thinking of that horrible nightmare. Then other brief dream scenes followed:

(1) ...a burning church in Alabama caused by a bomb explosion... three little girls killed in one of God's houses.

(2) ... a young Negro's body hanging from a tree limb with hooded villains, hiding under white sheets, strutting around a burning cross.

(3) ...my white, ministerial brother-in-law marching with Martin Luther King, Jr., surrounded by snaring police dogs and fire hoses and jeering sheetless KKK members.

(4) ...red necks stuck out of car windows shooting shot guns into homes of black Americans, just for the hell of it. I repeat, just for the HELL of it.

Then my dream scene shifted to the post office where my daughter works. She was wearing a safety mask and had on gloves. She was opening a suspicious looking little package.

"My God, anthrax!" I worried. She slowly and carefully opened the package. Thank God there was no white powder-like substance inside. However, the package contained a small wall hanging which read: **MUSLIM TERRORISTS ARE TO ISLAM WHAT THE KKK IS TO CHRISTIANITY.**

Fortunately, neither extreme, the Muslim terrorists nor the KKK members, represent the basic beliefs of either religion!!!

FATHER ABRAHAM

Last night I dream traveled to Jerusalem and then into the Dome of the Rock, that beautiful gold capped building that highlights the city's skyline. I took my shoes off because that is an Islamic custom. I put on a prayer cap because that is a Jewish custom. I then read from the New Testament because that is my custom.

Three different faiths with religious history in **one** place, I like that.

Three religions tracing their lineage through **one** man, Abraham. I like that also.

Three different groups of God sensitive people, searching to determine the will of the **same God**, though they call that Creator God by different names and approach this God via different rituals. I like that too.

For the **Jews,** the wailing wall is the remaining part of a temple built by their King Solomon. It housed their Ark. To them, it is very meaningful to place a written prayer in the cracks of this special wall and pray.

For the **Muslims,** Abraham demonstrated his undying faith by being submissive to God's testing. He was willing to sacrifice one of his sons on the rock which is inside their beautiful Islamic Dome.

For **Christians,** Jerusalem is the city where Jesus was nailed to a cross; where Jesus was somehow raised from an empty tomb; and where Jesus' resurrected Spirit inspired his cowardly disciples to bravely create a church! According to their St. Paul this Jesus is the Christ promised as Abraham's 'offspring'. (Galatians 3:16)

Again, **three different faiths revering the same place, the same man, and the same God.** I like that. I dreamed of that. I still dream of that.

Abraham and Moses
And
Jesus and Mohammed

In this dream, I observed a meeting among Abraham, Moses, Jesus and Mohammed.

Abraham spoke first: "Faith is the most important component of the spiritual journey."

Then **Moses** said: "To me, obeying the law, especially the Ten Commandments, is essential."

Jesus spoke next: "Keeping the faith and obeying the laws are important, but the personification of love is the key to happiness. That is, love for God who first loves us expressed in love for neighbor and love for self."

Mohammed declared: "Faith, obedience, love, these three are indeed key concepts of our Judeo-Christian-Islamic cultures; however, I am still convinced that submission to Allah's will is the primal concept to peace."

Again, **Abraham** spoke: "That is true, for by faith I left my homeland to follow Yahweh's will, and by faith I was willing to offer as a burnt offering one of my sons, only to discover human sacrifice was not Yahweh's will."

Moses took his turn: "You know, I like what the writer of Hebrews said about me; and I wish I had written his definition of faith before he did: 'Faith is the assurance of things hoped for, the conviction of things not seen.' (Hebrews 11:1)

Jesus turned to me and smiled warmly. I felt the challenge of what he was going to say next: "Let me give you an acronym. FAITH is Forsaking All, I Take Holiness. Holiness is the lacking attribute in most of today's religions. Holiness ascertains seeking to do God's will continually by obeying laws, doing justly, and sharing love actions."

Mohammed nodded approvingly, and then said: (As he gave Jesus a holy kiss) "Well said, Raboni. A holy life does integrate Allah's will, faith, obedience and love."

Then to my complete surprise, they joined in song singing as a quartet a harmonious rendition of King David's **Psalm 23**. It was absolutely beautiful:

"The Lord's my shepherd, I'll not want.
  He makes me down to lie
  in pastures green, He leadeth me the quiet waters by.
  Yea, though I walk in death's dark vale,
  yet will I fear no ill;
  for Thou art with me, and Thy rod and staff me comfort still.
  Goodness and mercy all my life shall surely follow me;
  and in God's house forevermore my dwelling place shall be."

And then, with a flash of brightness, the four visions disappeared. And as I have been instructed to do previously, I took up my pen and recorded this dream. **May Allah, Almighty God, and Yahweh be praised; and may these three names for the same Creator-creating God draw us closer together.**

Post-test on the Islamic Religion:

(Essay Test)

Write out two or three paragraphs about how Christians and Muslims could and should be able to coexist peacefully. Please stress the ideas these two major religions have in common.

CHRISTIANITY

AND

BUDDHISM

SOME EXCERPTS FROM THE TEACHING OF
THE BUDDHA

"You should respect each other, follow my teachings, and refrain from disputes; you should not, like water and oil, repel each other, but should, like milk and water, mingle together."

"Hatreds never cease by hatreds in this world. By love alone they cease. This is an ancient Law."

"Not to do any evil, To cultivate good, To purify one's mind - This is the advice of the Buddha."

"Your suffering is my suffering and your happiness is my happiness," said Buddha. "Just as a mother always loves her child, He does not forget that spirit even for a single moment. It is the nature of Buddhahood to be compassionate."

Buddha trained himself to avoid abusing others, and then he wished that all might have the serene mind that would follow by living in peace with others.

The Little Monk

His head was shaven. He wore a monk's robe and held his begging bowl in his left hand. Surprisingly, he was only about twelve years old.

"Hey kid," I called to him. "Come here a minute."

"Yes sir," he said as he approached me.

"I see you speak English," I said. "Good. Here is the deal: I will give you a hundred dollars if you can teach me your Eight Fold path. You see, I am very much interested in Buddhism, but I cannot seem to get it. Maybe I can understand it on a kid's level. How about it? Will you teach me what they have been teaching you at that school (monastery) you go to where you have been studying for your Bar mitzvah or confirmation or whatever.

"Not for money," he replied. "But I will try to teach you what I have learned about the Way for free." Of course I agreed. I had read that Buddhist are anti-materialistic; but I did not believe it. His refusal to take the hundred impressed me. He already had my undivided attention.

"First," my young tutor began, "Do you understand the **Four Noble Truths?**"

"Yes, I believe I do," I affirmed: "(1) Suffering is universal; (2) suffering is caused by desire; (3) one eliminates suffering by eliminating this desire; (4) you overcome desire by following the **Eight Fold Path**."

"Then you have probably noticed that the Buddha," the kid pointed out, "has tied the fourth noble truth into the first step of the Eight Fold Path. You see, the first step of the Eight Fold Path is right thinking; and right thinking for the Buddhist is to understand the Four Noble Truths.

The boy monk continued, "They also teach us the concepts of **impermanence** and **right mindfulness**. Impermanence meaning that everything is constantly changing; and mindfulness meaning being aware of the moment. They teach us the koan of the hungry bear chasing a monk off a cliff and his discovery of a flower halfway down meaning there will always be hungry bears in your path, but you can still enjoy the moment, if you have right thinking."

Step two is right intent. That is when we determine what we most want out of life. We are taught of the Buddha's refusing to live a life of wealth and leisure; and then six years later rejecting a life of poverty and extreme self-denial. He chose the middle way. You Americans would probably call this step the right motivation. Enlightenment is our goal. We do not want to be like a kite changing directions each time the wind's current shifts."

The youngster continued, "The next three steps are the action steps that control our lives: right speech, right conduct, and right actions. We are taught to analyze the things we say, to be calm and to be in charge through self discipline. We do not engage in idle chatter, or gossip, or slander or verbal abuse."

"Step four is right conduct. This step is taught in **five precepts;** similar to the Jewish Ten Commandments:
1) Do not kill or harm any living thing;
2) Do not steal;
3) Do not lie;
4) Do not be unchaste;
5) Do not drink intoxicants.
Right conduct or right action is like having two loaves of bread and exchanging one for a flower, while halving the remaining loaf and sharing it with the poor."

"Step five is right livelihood. That is choosing a job that promotes life instead of endangering or destroying it."

Then the young man interrupted his teaching to ask me if I had any questions. I was in awe of how well he was getting his points across. "So far, so good," I said. "Please continue."

He did: "The last three steps of the Eight Fold Path must be experienced rather than just explained. They come only from practicing meditation. The Buddha said, 'Those who follow the Way might well follow the example of the ox that marches through the deep mire carrying a heavy load. He is tired, but his steady, forward looking gaze will not relax until he comes out of the mire. Only then does he relax. O Monks, remember that passion and sin are more than the filthy mire, and that you can escape misery only by steadfastly preserving the Way'."

The twelve year old concluded: "They teach us at the monastery that only by this **right mindfulness** and **right concentrating** and **right effort** can we control our senses and emotions and urges."

I was speechless. Overwhelmed at the knowledge this kid had acquired. I stood there staring at him in amazement.

Smiling, my young tutor placed his palms together in a prayerful manner and bowed courteously to me. "I must be going," he said, "a lotus for you, a Buddhist to be."

Then as he mindfully breathed outwardly, it was as if his breath germinated a seed of understanding between us... and hopefully, between the Buddhist and the Christians (and all seekers) who may read this dream.

Fifty Times Fifty

It was one of those times when I was frustrated and confused about life and love and suffering and responsibilities and meaning. There was so much to do and so little time to do it in. In my attempt to sleep, I tossed and turned. Finally, I drifted off to dreamland in search of meaning.

In my dream, I stood before an enormous door that entered into a Buddhist monastery somewhere in Japan. I felt the answers to my quest were on the other side of that door. However, this was not a new dream for me. Many times before when I had been confused, I would dream of standing before this big, closed door. As I had done before, I knocked.

In the past visions, no one answered and I drifted off. This time I was determined to keep knocking until someone opened the door and talked with me.

Although time is relative in a dream, I stayed before the door all that day, and throughout that night. The next morning I knocked again, yelling that I was not leaving this time until someone opened the door. I sat there reading and pondering and praying and writing and engaging in Tai Chi exercises. That night I slept before the door again.

On the third day, a monk opened the door and greeted me warmly. "Why did it take you so long to open the blessed door?" I demanded.

"It did not seem long at all to us," he stated. "Then too, we wanted to make sure you were serious."

"Well, I guess that makes sense," I replied. "But I wasted three days of my life waiting."

"Not necessarily," the greeter monk argued. "But then, that might just be a symptom of your problems. So what brings you to our monastery? What are you seeking?"

I began: "I want you to help me better understand suffering. I acknowledge the wisdom of the Enlightened One's Eight Fold Path for right living, and I know that the Buddha exemplified his belief by giving up his earthly kingdom. But human suffering disturbs my belief system."

The Buddhist priest closed his eyes, opened his palms skyward, and said, "Fast during Ramadan and/or lent, and thus increase your appreciation of life. Visit a hospital and befriend and minister to a sick and terminal patient. Support a widow or console a woman who has been raped or a young boy who has been sexually victimized as I was as a child. You do not find the answer by thinking about suffering. You find the answer by leaving your palace, whatever that may be, and by exchanging clothing with the have-nots (at least figuratively) and identifying with the poor, the old and the sickly as did the Buddha."

Then the spirit-filled young man opened his eyes and looking directly into mine, he asked, "Do you remember Jesus' encounter with the rich young ruler? That young man had the right answers, but he only knew about suffering. He did not know suffering. What your bible does not tell you is that within the year, that rich young ruler caught leprosy, spent all of his wealth seeking a cure, and/or because no one associated with him, lost his business relationships and finally joined a group of ten lepers."

"Again, he made his way to Jesus. He was the one leper of the ten who returned to thank Jesus, because he had learned the meaning of suffering by suffering. As have I, as a victimized youth, he became a wounded healer. Your personal suffering and pain should cause you to do the same. But even if you cannot give everything to the poor, at least tell this story to your readers."

The Buddhist priest concluded: "Through suffering, and/or being around suffering, one can achieve Nirvana or one can walk away from suffering and just keep on asking the question, 'Why do people have to suffer?' The statistics of the Jesus story are about right. Even nine out of ten of those who do suffer do not understand or appreciate their opportunity. Suffering is universal. But sufferers can convert pain to beautiful attitudes, ignorance to enlightenment, suffering to hopeful endurance, and failure to creative living."

After helping me to better understand suffering, the greeter monk invited me to take a seat with the others for a concert by a guest performer. And was I ever surprised. Sister Betty Smith, from the mountains of North Carolina, my home state, was about to sing some mountain ballads. The monk whispered: "Listen carefully. You just might find the words of her ballads to be pertinent to your situation."

These are the words to Mrs. Smith's ballad:

"There once was an owl, perched on a shed;
  Fifty years later, the owl was dead.
  Fifty times fifty, and the years go by,
  Corn keeps best when it's cool and dry;
  And fifty times fifty and one by one,
  Night begins when the day is done."

"Some say mice are in the corn,
  Some say kittens are being born,
  Some say a kitten becomes a cat,
  Mice are likely to know about that."

"Some cats are scratchy, and some are not;
  Corn grows best when it's damp and hot.
  Owl on the shed, cat in the clover;
  Mice in the corn, and it all starts over."

"Fifty times fifty and one by one,
  Night begins when the day is done."

When the concert was over, the monks applauded with their
aditional one hand ovation, standing to honor the aged singer
f folk ballads. Mrs. Smith had a beautiful smile on her face as
he stood before the applauding monks. She took her bows; and
en grasped her chest. Her body slumped to the floor.

A previously unnoticed old owl which had been looking
own from it's perch on a nearby shed flew away as if with her
oul. The Persian cat, resting by the fire, continued to sleep as
er kittens played spiritedly near her.

Mrs. Smith's body was covered and removed. Then everyone left me sitting there alone. Nothing else needed to be said. They all knew I would be sitting there the rest of the day, pondering and reading and praying and writing and engaging in Tai Chi exercises. They knew that I had learned that time is indeed, relative.

I picked up Mrs. Smith's dulcimer and gently placed it across my lap. As I strummed it softly, I sang:

> "Owl on the shed, cat in the clover,
>   Mice in the corn, and it all starts over.
>   Fifty times fifty, and one by one,
>   Night begins when the day is done."

A Zen Dream

Zen Buddhism places importance on living fully in the now. For Zen, nothing is of greater value than the moment. This is the point of the Buddhist koan I read just before I retired for the night. I have copied it for you to read:

"There was a Buddhist monk who one day found himself running from a hungry bear. The bear chased him off a cliff. There was nothing for him to do, if he did not desire to be food for the bear's hungry stomach, but jump. He did so and was able to catch hold, as he fell, of a branch of wood growing from the cliff's side. As he hung there, looking up at the hungry bear above, he heard the roar of a famished lion far below who was already waiting for him to tire, lose his grip and fall into it's hungry jaws."

"As the monk hung suspended, hungry bear above and starving lion below, he noticed the heads of two gophers on the small stump of wood to which he clung so desperately."

"All at once the monk saw that just a stretch away was a small clump of wild strawberries. He calmly reached out, plucked the largest, reddest, and ripest of the berries, and put it to his mouth. 'How delicious!' he said."

Now here is my dream for that night:

"I was running from a hungry bear. He chased me off a cliff. Half way down I grabbed hold of a protruding root and held on for dear life."

"Under me I saw a starving lion. A gopher appeared and started gnawing the root. Then I noticed a patch of wild berries within my reach. I selected the next to the ripest one and offered it to the gopher. As he reached for the berry, I knocked him off the cliff and into the starving lion's mouth. The lion seemed satisfied and left the area. Then I ate the best berry and dropped safely to the ground."

"Looking up at the growling bear, I yelled: 'You better be glad I did not have my shot gun with me this time. But I will be looking for you at bear hunting season, big fellow. The good Lord willing, you are going to make a nice rug to go before my fireplace. Until then, I suggest that you enjoy every precious minute.'"

Thus, a Zen dream, stressing the importance of the moment; with a little western Protestantism added.

My Only Daughter

In this dream, my only daughter came home from college and announced: "Mom, Dad, great news! I am in love with a wonderful man. He has asked me to marry him. He is a Japanese exchange student. He is Buddhist. He is cute as a button; has got a wonderful personality; and I love him dearly. Please say you approve. I am so happy."

"Wait now, hold on a minute," I stalled. "We haven't even met him yet. But if you have come to love him, we know that he is sensitive and sensible. Feel assured that we will meet him more than half way."

Her Mom responded: "Congratulations honey. You seem so excited. We are shocked; but very happy for you."

"Thanks Mom," our daughter said joyfully, as she embraced her mother. Then she looked back at me and asked: "Dad?"

"A Buddhist?" I redirected.

"You will love him Dad. He is a lot like you. He is relaxed and confident and intelligent. And you already have something in common," she informed me.

"And what might that be?" I asked.

"You both love me," she yelled as she ran into my arms and hugged me happily.

"And Dad, " she continued as she took a step backwards to look into my eyes (a tactic I remembered I had taught her) "Since you teach world religions at the community college, we want you to prepare two lists for us. One of important Buddhist terms for me to learn; and one of Christian terms for Jap (evidently, Jap was an acceptable, positive nick name for him). You see, we have love for each other, and if we can just communicate that love with understanding, then we feel we can work out our religious and cultural differences. What do you think Dad? Will you do it?"

"That is a great idea, young lady," I agreed. "A good way to better understand a different religion is to learn the vocabulary. You need to learn about zen; and he needs to learn about sin," I laughed alone. Bad joke.

"Oh, and Dad, Mom," she blurted out. "One other thing. We are going to live in Japan."

"No!" I begged as I awakened abruptly. I was most pleased that I had been dreaming. However after recording this dream, I decided to suggest the two lists of vocabulary terms, for just maybe, it is time for Buddhist and Christians to marry.

List for Christians:	**List for Buddhist:**
Four Noble Truths	Original Sin
Eightfold Path	Atonement
Five Precepts	Conversion

List for Christians:	List for Buddhists:
Three Divine Virtues	Justification by Faith
Impermanence	Stewardship
Right Mindfulness	Discipleship
Non-attachment	Will of God
Non-violence	Love of God
Selflessness	Love of Neighbor
Dispassionate	Savior
Anti-materialistic	Lord
Karma	Redeemer
Nirvana	Comforter
Reincarnation	Trinity
Interbeing	Sacraments
Koan	Son of God
Reverance for All Life	God's Grace

Only Passing Through !

In this dream,

    I saw **Adam** and **Eve** leave their garden
        with apples in their hands…
    I asked: "Now that you are out,
        what are you guys going to do?"

    Adam said: "Plant our crops and pray for rain,
        and maybe raise a 'little Cain';
           for there is so little time,
        and we are only passing through."

    I saw **Noah** in that ark.
        For forty days he couldn't park.
    I asked: "Captain Noah,
        why is that rainbow in the sky?"

    He said: "Continue to ask the question, 'Why?'
        for sooner or later, we all must die!
    There is so little time, we're only passing through."

    I saw **Abraham** carry one of his son's up a hill,
        submitting to Yahweh's holy will.
    "Where is the sacrifice you are going to kill?"

    He said: "Have complete faith in God
        in everything you say and do;
    For there is so little time,
        and you are only passing through."

I saw **David** kill that giant;
 and then, for lust, become defiant.
I asked: 'King David, what is that psalm you sing?"

 He said: "Sing your psalms of praise and glory,
  as you personalize your own spiritual story.
   for there is so little time,
    and we are only passing through."

I saw the **Buddha** sitting under his tree,
 Pondering 'suffering' for you and me.
 I asked: "Have you found the path, O Noble One?"

 He said: "The middle way; and the victory is won;
  but there is so little time,
   before your earthly life is done."

I saw **Jesus** on that tree, on a hill called Calvary.
"Do you hate mankind for what we have done to you?"

 He said: "Speak of love, and not of hate…
  Things to do, it's getting late…
 There is so little time, you are only passing through."

Next, I stood before the prophet **Mohammed.**
 I asked: "What would you have us do?"

He said: "Allah's will be done; treat all brothers as one;
 and praise God's holy name in everything you do.

For there is so little time; and we are only passing through!"

I saw **Mother Teresa** doing her chores,
  cleaning the wounds of a leper's sores.
  "How could you dare do this?" I asked.

She said: "Because of love, it's not a task;
for only what's done for God will last.
Our earthly life will soon be past.
There is so little time, and time passes very fast."

I felt **God** had spoken to me,
  for through this dream God helped me see...

"Whether Muslim, Christian, Buddhist or Jew,
  'Kindly Acts' are the right things to do."

There is so little time, and we are only passing through.

One God

In this dream, I audit a conference among: Abraham, Moses, Buddha, Jesus and Mohammad. Mohammad speaks first.

Mohammad: "A point of clarity Abraham. We Muslims believe you were going to offer Ishmael as a burnt offering and the Jews and Christians teach that it was Isaac. Which son was it?"

Abraham: "'Which son' is not the important issue. 'Neither son' is the important result. Our God did not require human sacrifice like the neighboring tribes around us did at that time. This was a major step of spiritual growth for a primitive religion. And speaking of spiritual growth, Moses, I wonder if your ten commandments are still relevant. For instance, no one in the modern world worships idols. Isn't your second commandment out dated?"

Moses: "Have you observed the latest models of automobiles, the three story mansions, the things the 21st century people rush about to collect? Of course my commandment about 'graven images' is still relevant. And I might add, so are the other nine."

Jesus: "Moses, I took your ten commandments out of the negative 'thou shalt nots' and made a positive statement: 'You shall love God, and love your neighbor as yourself'. But yes, your 2nd commandment is still relevant. The prayer I taught the Christians was asking God to give them their 'daily bread'; not a big bank account. My emphasis was on loving people and using things. Too many moderns seem to be using people and loving things."

71

Buddha: "I too stressed the impermanence of things. And I have noticed that some modern Christians seem to be living for a pie-in-the-sky-bye-and-bye. It seems to me the goal should be to share the pie now; particularly with the third world have-nots."

Mohammed: "Agreed. So many well to do Americans have confused Christianity with democracy. Democracy is not a religion; it is a form of government. And the Golden Rule is not 'He who has the gold makes the rules!'

Moses: "Most politicians, world leaders of every country, misspeak and comprise their principles and accept favors for their influence. My ninth commandment still holds: 'Thy shalt not bear false witness.'"

Buddha: "Following Jesus' example, let's see if we can make a positive statement about peaceful co-existence among all religions and tolerance of our differences. Anybody?"

Abraham: "It seems to me that there is one major thing on which we all agree. We each experienced the 'call' of the One, the Creator God."

Moses: "Yes, we Jews call it the Shema: 'Hear. O Israel, the Lord thy God is... ONE ...'"

Jesus: "The secret to experiencing God's presence and understanding His will is prayer. Many times I rose before dawn and spent private, precious moments talking and listening to God in order to determine His will. Prayer is paramount."

Mohammad: "We Muslims pray five times a day and I agree, prayer is the secret to determining Allah's will."

Moses: "At the burning bush, when I took my shoes off because I was on holy ground, I felt Yahweh's presence."

Buddha: "When I was meditating under the Buddha tree, I experienced enlightenment and an awareness of Power and Creative Energy which you monotheists no doubt call God."

Abraham: "Then we all pretty much agree. There is one Creator-Creating God whom we call by different names; but with Whom we each have communicated with through prayer and/or meditation. Let us conclude then: 'There is One God!' And our spiritual objective should be to feel an awareness of and to try to determine the will of this... **One God.**"

Jesus: "Ours is to help people to realize a God-consciousness."

Post-test on Buddhism

Matching:

1. Impermanence ___   A) Not harming any living thing

2. Right Mindfulness ___   B) A state of perfect peace

3. Koan ___   C) A meditation exercise

4. Suffering ___   D) ... is universal

5. Right Intent ___   E) How to end "desire"

6. Nirvana ___   F) Everything is constantly
                               changing

7. Reverence for Life___   G) Determining what one wants
                               most out of life

8. Tai Chi ___   H) A Buddhist parable

9. Enlightenment ___   I) Under the Buddha Tree

10. Four Noble Truths ___   J) Being aware of the moment

CHRISTIANITY

AND

DENOMINATIONS

SOME EXCEPTS FROM THE NEW TESTAMENT

"One of the scribes came near and heard them disputing with one another, and seeing that he answered them well, he asked him, 'Which commandment is the first of all?' Jesus answered: *The first is, 'Hear O Israel, the Lord our God, the Lord is ONE; you shall love the Lord your God with all your heart, and with all your soul, and with all your mind, and with all your strength.' The second is this: 'You shall love your neighbor as yourself.' There is no other commandment greater than these." (Mark 12: 28-31)*

Jesus preaches: "This is my commandment. 'That you love one another as I have loved you.'" (John 15:12)

Jesus prays: "Holy Father…may they be **one,** as we are **one.** I ask not only on behalf of these, but also on behalf of those who will believe in me through their word, that they may all be **one.** (John 17:20)

Paul teaches: "Is God the God of Jews only? Is He not the God of Gentiles also? Yes, of Gentiles also. Since God is **…ONE…**" (Romans 3:25)

Paul reiterates: "…with all humility and gentleness, with patience, bearing with one another in love, making every effort to maintain the unity of the Spirit in the bond of peace…there is **One God** and Father of all…" (Ephesians 4:2-6)

Disagreements Among Early Christians

A few years after the death of Jesus, a man named Barnabas ed an active congregation of Christian believers in Antioch, a ty located a few miles north of Jerusalem. His church was ntegrated and mission oriented. Pastor Barnabas invited Paul, 1 ex-persecutor of the Christians, recently converted to the ith, to be his assistant. (Acts 11:19-27}.

Barnabas, Paul, and a young man named John Mark were ommissioned by the Antioch church to embark on a uissionary journey to the island of Cyprus. For whatever :ason, the young man left the mission team before the project ·as completed. His untimely departure caused a disagreement etween Barnabas, who wanted to give John Mark a second hance and take him with them on their next missionary ›urney; and Paul who refused to give him another opportunity. he result: church mathematics - divide and multiply. arnabas and John Mark went back to Cyprus; and Paul and is new associate, Silas, went to a different area of service. **wo outstanding Christians disagreeing on an issue.**

Another issue of disagreement among early Christians - iould new converts be required to be circumcised? The Jewish hristians in Jerusalem, led by James, Jesus' brother, said ´es'. After their first missionary journey to Cyprus, Barnabas id Paul said 'No'.

A conference was called in Jerusalem to settle the issue. At ie conference, Peter told of a recurring dream he had received ›out accepting gentiles into the church and how he had been instrumental in the conversion of a Roman officer. The group voted to not require neophytes to be circumcised as an initiation ritual. Thus, freeing Christianity from becoming a sect of Judaism. **This is another example of early Christians disagreeing on an issue.**

Even though Peter had swayed the Jerusalem conference with his testimony to accept gentile converts as uncircumcised equals, once when visiting Antioch, Peter refused to eat with the gentiles and chose to eat only with the Jewish guest visitors from Jerusalem. This act of segregation upset Paul and they argued. Paul, the new convert, dared to challenge Peter, chosen by Jesus as one of the twelve disciples. **Two outstanding, early Christians disagreeing over an issue.**

Although Paul got the best of the argument in Antioch, Peter seems to have gotten the last word when he is quoted in II Peter 3: 15-16... "there are some things in them (Paul's letters) hard to understand." A statement with which I readily agree.

In a dream which I will not detail, but only mention that I dared to confront Paul about Women's rights and Gay rights, Paul concluded that times change, and therefore Christians must continue to discuss issues. And so it is - the dialogue goes on. **Christians disagree on some issues, and should.**

St. Paul on Denominations

e: "Thank you Paul for appearing in this dream about co-
eration among denominations. I was just reading in one of
ur letters you wrote to Corinth these very appropriate words:

'For as long as there is jealousy and quarreling
among you, are you not of the flesh, and behav-
ing according to human inclinations? For when
one says, "I belong to Paul," and another says,
"I belong to Apollos," are you not merely human?
... I planted, Apollos watered, but God gave the
growth!' (I Corinthians 3:5-6)

If I may paraphrase you, today some say they are Baptist;
d others say they are Methodist; but we are all following
rist. Do you think that is a relevant statement?"

ul: "Yes, of course. And I remind you of my letter to the
hesians: 'There is one body and one Spirit, just as you were
lled to the one hope of your calling, one Lord, one faith...
ne God and Father of all, who is above all and through all
d in all.'" (Ephesians 4:4-6)

e: "By the way Paul, in Acts 20:35, Luke quotes you as
ying that Jesus said, **'It is more blessed to give than to
ceive'.** I cannot find that text anywhere in the four Gospels."

ul: "You must remember that the Gospels had not been
itten when I preached. I was surprised that Luke did not
clude that saying in his Gospel. I learned of the saying from
hat you scholars today call the oral tradition period. The

phrase was quite popular in my day and was passed down by word of mouth."

Me: "Also, when you preached, the Temple was still standing in Jerusalem and animal sacrifice was most meaningful. Today, few people understand such a concept of animal sacrifice as a substitution atonement (Jesus' crucifixion as the Lamb of God) If you were preaching today, wouldn't you have used a different initiation ritual, say the marriage ceremony. It seems to me that saying 'I do' accept God as my life's partner would be much better than saying, 'Jesus died for my sins,' or 'I'm saved by the blood of the Lamb of God,' or even, 'I've been born again'."

Paul: "Well, you know I never married. So that pretty much rules out that idea." Paul laughed. "And my opinion of women keeping silent in church has always been criticized. In my day and time women were uneducated and unemployed outside the home. I am sure if I lived in your day, I would be impressed differently about the ability of professional, educated women. And about the 'rebirth' or 'born again' concept, I realize now that even Nicodemus, the teacher of the Pharisees, had trouble with that idea." (John 3:1-21)

Me: "Incidentally, **that is the only time Jesus uses that term, 'born again'; and the phrase appears only one more time in the entire New Testament** (1st Peter 1:22-23). **Also, it is interesting to me that his blood had not been shed when he offers Nicodemus eternal life**. Doesn't that repudiate the 'blood of Jesus washes away my sins' theory? And another topic I think you might make a different statement about is homosexuality. You called that life-style 'not natural'; but modern science has proven that it is quite natural for about every one out of ten."(Romans 1:20)

Paul: "Let's go back to the substitution atonement theory and let me try to clarify. My major point was that one could not earn a place in heaven. Heaven is now awarded by the grace of God to those who accept Jesus Christ as Lord and Savior and Messiah. Perhaps John said it best some fifty years after my death, 'For God so loved the world that He gave His only begotten Son, so that everyone who believes in Him may not perish but have eternal life'." (John 3:16)

Me: "Amen, but can one not believe in Jesus without the thought: 'He died for us'? I prefer the thought: 'He lived and loved and died because of his teachings against the way the Romans treated their captives. I believe Jesus' major contribution was not dying for us, but living a life of love for us to demonstrate how God wishes us to live. Jesus taught and exemplified the love principle expressed in love for God, neighbor and self. I stressed Christian ethics in my preaching."

Paul: "You make a good point Brother Starnes. Christian nurture is very important, but before one can grow in the faith, one must first make a decision to become a Christian. My calling was to travel throughout the known world and establish house churches, filling them with proselyte Jews and previously considered 'unclean' Gentiles."

Me: "Over the years, these little house churches that you started Paul, have grown and grouped and organized and adopted different rituals and varying creeds. But whether Messianic Jew or Gentile, Catholic or Protestant, or whatever the denomination or on whatever the continent, the important ingredients to harmonious co-operation among God seekers are what you called the fruits of the Spirit: '**love, joy, peace, kindness, generosity, faithfulness, gentleness, and self-control.**' (Galatians 5:22)

Paul: "Since we began this dream with a quote from my letters to Corinth, let us conclude this dream discussion in like manner. As I wrote in my love chapter (1st Corinthians 13) 'Now abideth faith, hope and love, these three. But the **greatest of all is love'**."

Me: "Thank you Paul. Well said. Will you now pronounce a benediction for my readers?"

Paul: "Certainly. 'Almighty God, may brother Starnes' readers be inspired by this book to become more tolerant, accepting of others, ecumenical, loving and peaceful. May they understand that everyone they meet is loved by You, Creator-Creating God; and that they too should look for and encourage those loveable things that are in everyone, although hard to find in some. In the name of love, truth and beauty I pray this. Amen.'"

Jesus Speaks to a 1st Century Christian
And to a 21st Century Christian

After reading the opening chapter of John's gospel, I retired for the evening. Within the hour, I was standing on the banks of the Jordan River, observing as John the Baptizer pointed out the 'Lamb of God' to Andrew and another disciple.

Two things puzzled me as I tried to catch the mood of the occasion:

(1) First, what did John the Baptist... the wild one, the wilderness wonder, the camel hair wearing, grass hopper eating prophet... know about 'sacrificial lambs'?

Then I remembered that before John left home and took to the wilderness that his daddy was a Jewish priest. Who better than one who had been raised in the home of a Jewish priest to announce Jesus as the 'Lamb of God'? The family would have been very familiar with the custom of animal sacrifice.

(2) The second thing that bothered me about my text fulfilling dream was that the two men were not Andrew and his famous brother, Peter, but Andrew and John (perhaps the author of the gospel that bares his name). I deduced that John was the other unnamed disciple because of his writing style of never identifying himself by name. Also, the teller of this first chapter story takes one to the exact time, 4 p.m., and place of his encounter with Jesus. Many new converts can do that today. Why else would John have given the time of day? (Please see chapter one of the gospel of John for this complete story. It is beautifully written.)

Then Jesus spoke in my dream and my mind really began to think deeply. "What do you want? He asked. As he elaborated, my mind raced: **"What do you want out of life? What do you hope to accomplish? For what are you living? What really matters to you?"**

Andrew responded out loud as if only he and Jesus were there. He worded: "I guess 'fish' are the most important things in my life. I have really never seriously thought of it before, and that is sad, but I eat, sleep, and think 'fish'; and that is even sadder. We start early in the morning and stay at it all day long, every day of our lives, except the Sabbath."

"Have you ever thought about becoming a fisher of men?" the Christ-figure asked. "Why don't you go get your brother and let's explore that possibility? I am putting together a group of men to work as a mission team to preach and teach and heal and to saturate the Lake Galilee area with the idea of a New Kingdom concept, a fellowship of believers in spiritual things that are far more important than just 'eating, sleeping and thinking fish'. We are going to be thinking salvation, and spiritual maturity for both men and women, and discipleship in the Kingdom of God."

Andrew nodded agreeingly; and took off to look for his big brother Simon, who later would become Peter, the 'Rock'."

Then Jesus looked directly into John's eyes and asked him specifically, but I felt he was talking to me indirectly: "What are your strengths young man? What would you really like to do to help make this a better world? What is the one thing you feel you can contribute to this ministry?"

"I enjoy writing," John spoke up, and it was as if he was speaking for both of us, for I too enjoy writing.

John continued: "I would like to record what you just told Andrew about becoming a fisher of men. I'd like to keep a record of your ministry so that others may learn of your teachings. Perhaps I can write up some of your parables and things of interest so that even our children and maybe even their children can learn of your teachings about love and help and salvation. I just enjoy writing, and I enjoy being in your presence."

Then Jesus smiled contentedly and turned and looked into my eyes and said: "Then write... write what you feel, what you dream, what you believe will help make a better world."

I awakened, feeling the responsibility and the courage to pick up my pen and to write what I feel, what I believe, what I had just dreamed...

Catholics and Protestants

This dream is about a little German monk who said, "I just cannot!" to the mighty Pope Leo X of Rome in 1521.

Me: "**Martin Luther,** I presume," as I tried to identify my night visitor.

M.L.: "And who might ye be who hast caused me to appeareth before him in this dream?" he asked in fifteenth/sixteenth century dialect and attire. (A strange accent I thought, but I was pleased that he did not speak in his native tongue, German, because I do not know that language.)

I answered: "Just an insignificant twentieth/twenty-first century protestant preacher who stands as lowly before you as you probably felt standing before the Pope's legate at Worms in 1521."

M.L.: "Ye need not feel intimidated, my fellow protestant clergyman, for whatever century you liveth, as it was in the first century, **the foot of the cross is level.** All men standeth equal before God... be they pope or priest or preacher or layman; be they carpenter or miner's son or scholar or mother or king."

Me: "The priesthood of all believers," I questioned?

M.L.: "Exactly," he confirmed.

Me: "And you are no doubt referring to yourself as that miner's son? I wonder, did your father ever forgive you for not becoming the lawyer he sent you to school to become?"

M.L.: "No, he truly did not. He left this world believing my divine call to be a monk was just an accidental bolt of lightning, which he called the devil's spook," Luther smiled.

Me: "Your call was similar to St. Paul's, was it not?"

M.L.: "To be sure, and it is to St. Paul that I owe my spiritual awakening. For I discovered in reading Paul's letter to Rome that the "just shall live by faith;" and not by men's achievements.

Me: Again I questioned: "The doctrine of the justification by faith which became the principle foundation for the Reformation."

Again Rev. Luther confirmed: "Exactly; and permit me to help you maketh your third principle. My hope was no longer in the pope; but in the recognition of the Holy Bible as the sole authority in religious matters."

Me: "Brother Martin, will you speak a little more about the Council at Worms?"

M.L.: "Would to God I could have recanted on that day. I wished a reformation; not a repudiation. But I could not. What I had written in my books, was written in my heart and I could not retract and recall them and their contents."

Me: "I have read your open letter to the Pope Leo X, and your devotional you sent with it entitled: 'The Freedom of the Christian Man'. I have also read your 'Explanations of the Ninety-five Theses' and I agree. You could not recant. But fortunately for you and for the future of the protestant movement, Germany was ready to also say 'No' to the distant Italian influence and drain of her money to the Pope in Rome. Therefore, you could become a live hero instead of a dead heretic."

M.L.: "Yes, and though I did not know it at the time, I was later to enjoy a happy and serene married life, nurturing six children. And thanks to the invention of the printing press, I was able to publish my sermons and devotional readings in the languages of the people for the next twenty years."

M.L., sensing a conclusion to my dream, continues: "But you are correct, dreamer, the three main factors of the Reformation are:

(1) the authority of the Holy Bible,
(2) the justification by faith,
(3) the priesthood of all believers.

Me: "Thank you for appearing in my dream. I shall always have a special feeling now when I hear our church sing 'A Mighty Fortress is Our God' by Martin Luther."

M.L.: "I thanketh thou, but it would please me that thou knoweth that I also wrote the children's Christmas carol:

'Ah, dearest Jesus, Holy Child,
Make Thee a bed, soft, and undefiled
Within my heart, that it may be,
A quit chamber fit for Thee.'

I awoke thinking: "A mighty fortress is our God, who wishes to be born into the hearts of all His beloved children, who have been justified by faith."

Note from the dreamer-author: "Like all of us, Martin Luther had his good qualities and his bad. Among his bad was his anti-Semitism. For whatever reasons, Luther hated the Jews. The following is a copy of a pamphlet he wrote in 1543.

On the Jews and their Lies
By Martin Luther

What shall we Christians do with this rejected and condemned people, the Jews? I shall give you my sincere advice.

First: Set fire to their synagogues or schools and bury and cover with dirt whatever will not burn, so that no man will ever again see a stone or cinder of them.

Second: I advise that their homes also be razed and destroyed for they pursue in them the same aims as in their synagogues.

Third: I advise that all their prayer books and Talmudic writings, in which such adultery, lies, cursing and blasphemy are taught, be taken from them.

Fourth: I advise that their Rabbis be forbidden to teach hence-forth on pain of loss of life and limb.

Fifth: I advise that safe conduct on the highways be abolished completely for the Jews.

Sixth: I advise that all cash and treasure of silver and gold be taken from them.

Seventh: Let whoever can, throw brimstone and pitch upon them, so much the better, and if this be not enough, let them be driven like mad dogs out of the land.

Note from the Author: "Years later, his fellow German country man, Adolf Hitler, implemented Luther's advice with the horrible Holocaust disgrace. Conversely, the Church Council of the Evangelical Lutheran Church of America on April 18, 1994, adopted the following document as an apology to the Jewish people and as a statement on Lutheran/Jewish relations.

Declaration of the Evangelical Lutheran Church in America to the Jewish Community

The Lutheran communion of faith is linked by name and heritage to the memory of Martin Luther, teacher and reformer. Honoring his name in our own, we recall his bold stand for truth, his earthy and sublime words of wisdom, and above all his witness to God's saving Word. Luther proclaimed a gospel for people as we really are, bidding us to trust a grace sufficient to reach our deepest shames and address the most tragic truths.

In the spirit of that truth-telling, we who bear his name and heritage must with pain acknowledge also Luther's anti-Judaic diatribes and violent recommendations of his later writings against the Jews. As did many of Luther's own companions in the sixteenth century, we reject this violent invective, and yet more do we express our deep and abiding sorrow over its tragic effects on subsequent generations...moreover, we express our urgent desire to live out our faith in Jesus Christ with love and respect for the Jewish people... Finally, we pray for the continued blessing of the Blessed One upon the increasing cooperation and understanding between Lutheran Christians and the Jewish community,

One More Note from the Dreamer-Author

"How **horrible** of the Catholic Church, an attempt to increase their riches by the selling of indulgencies to the ignorant poor in order to release their deceased loved ones from a purgatory.

How **wonderful,** the courage of Martin Luther to speak out against the selling of these indulgencies with the ninety five thesis.

How **horrible,** the anti-Jewish advice Martin Luther wrote in his pamphlet: "On The Jews and Their Lies".

How **beautiful,** the insightfulness of the contemporary Lutheran Church to apologize for their founder and to reach out to today's Jewish people in Christ-like love.

How **hopeful,** that Catholics and Lutherans and Jews can respect the beliefs of the others, and **that we all can live harmoniously and co-operatively together.**

Pope John Paul, II

It was while Pope John Paul, II was visiting Mexico and the United States, that I received this papal dream. The pope was then 78, hobbled by ill health and shaking visibly as he sat in a chair in my bedroom.

"Your holiness," I respectfully greeted him. "I am deeply moved that you have appeared to me in this dream. Pray tell me the message that you wish for me to record in my book."

He spoke very softly, in English, "That rich and poor nations and people of all faiths should unite to end poverty and all forms of social discrimination; and that young people should lead the way."

"Sir," I stated quite excitedly, "I too have seen the masses of poor and the results of poverty in and around Mexico City. I have worshipped both at the Catholic cathedral on Zocolo Square and at the Shrine of the Virgin of Guadaloupe. It was outside that shrine that I saw an incident that I shall never forget… a young couple on their bleeding knees, praying their way down the street to the church. I also saw a mystical, subliminal image of the Christ in a secular mural by Diego Rivera on the wall of the capital. But please forgive me for talking when I should be listening. What can I do to help you, God being my helper?"

His holiness again spoke ever so softly, "At times people have refused to respect and love their brothers and sisters of a different race or faith; they have denied fundamental rights to individuals and nations."

After that lamentation, he reiterated: "As a writer, I want you to **emphasize that rich and poor nations and people of all faiths should unite to end poverty and all forms of social discriminations, and that the young people should lead the way.**"

As I awakened the pope blessed me with the sign of the cross; and then vanished. I quickly rose and recorded this brief, but most important dream... a dream of people of all faiths, cooperating, listening to each other, sharing with each other, and serving others (particularly the poor and those who are discriminated against).

A Protestant Preacher

In A Confessional Booth

In this dream I find myself standing before three confessional booths in a Roman Catholic Church. I was waiting for my friend, Father Charlie Goodson, to finish hearing the confessionals; and then we were going to lunch.

Charlie opened the door of the middle booth and greeted me with his usual warm smile and hand shake. "Glad you are here," he said. "I've got to go to the men's room. Do me a favor. Sit in the booth until I get back. You've heard me talk about it so much, you know how to do the penances. Anyway, seldom does one come this time of morning. Go ahead. Get in. I'll be right back and we will go to lunch."

I had no more closed the door to the middle booth when someone opened the door of the booth to my left, and then almost simultaneously, someone entered the confessional booth to my right.

There I sat as a protestant minister, hearing the confessionals of two men at the same time. I'd listen to one for a while, then asked him to say a rosary while I would listen to the other.

Now here's the even more fascinating thing: both men were worried about relationships with their lovers. Both spoke of trust vs. mistrust, of friendship and kindness and of mutual respect, of commitment and compassionate caring. Then to my surprise, I discovered one was gay and the other heterosexual.

Whether male/female, or same gender relationship, the important components are not sex organs. A mutually satisfying, 'happy', growth encouraging relationship depends very little on whether the couple has two penises, or one penis and one vagina, or two vaginas. Needless to say, I was very glad when Father Goodson reappeared.

ECUMENISM

He boasted that he was two things, "I am a Republican and a Baptist!"

His companion added, "Actually Joe, you are three things. You are a Republican, a Baptist, and a 'son of a bitch'."

Needless to say Joe's buddy was a Democrat and a Methodist. However, both Democrats and Republicans are Americans; and both Baptist and Methodist are Christian. Shouldn't American Christians get along? **And in keeping with the purpose of this book, shouldn't Universal religions co-exist peacefully and co-operatively?**

If I am correct, most Baptist still insist on an emersion baptism, while Methodist sprinkle. Some denominations claim "once saved, always saved," while other denominations recognize "back sliding." Presbyterians are noted for their belief in predestination. All Episcopalians are thought to be well-to-do and educated. Church of Goders, for their speaking in tongues. And the differences go on…

But what does it really matter? **The label on the outside of the jar is not as important as the content of that jar.** In essence, the compassion Jesus had for all people (especially the poor), the love he expressed through his parabolic teaching, his willingness to sacrifice his life for his beliefs… these are the central and important issues of Christianity. The peculiarities of the different denominations are really a side issue.

As far as denominations are concerned, the question is not are you a Baptist or a Methodist or a Catholic; rather the question becomes are you a Christ-o-centric person. Do your values coincide with the teachings and example of Jesus Christ, no matter where you choose to worship.

Incidentally, Jesus stressed prayer as a wonderful medium by which one experiences an increased awareness of God's presence and power. He taught us, his disciples, to pray: "Our Father;" not just "My Father". "Our" is a collective, plural pronoun. It implies a "We-ness", a company of believers; even more than a denomination. **We are a family under One God.**

Therefore, brothers and sisters of the faith, let the Christian Baptist and the Christian Methodist and the Christian Presbyterians join hands as followers of the Christ-like way. One can be ecumenical in thought and still maintain one's individual choice of denominations… **if one respects the rights of others to have that same choice.** (Hope you readers will forgive an old preacher for preaching a little.)

Now to the dream. I call this dream: 'Three Dreams about Peter's Three Dreams'. In the tenth chapter of Dr. Luke's second book, Acts, Peter receives a recurring dream. Three times he experiences the same vision. (Acts 11:1-18)

I have found that a recurring dream usually suggests that the dream recipient is struggling with a difficult decision. In Peter's case, the struggle was whether or not to baptize gentiles.

After deciding that God was instructing him via these

97

dreams, Peter dared to break the norm and baptized Cornelius, a Roman centurion. And thus Christianity went universal; not to remain a Jewish sect. What a momentous decision, influenced greatly by Peter's dreams.

The following are three of my dreams about Peter's three dreams: (Please read about Peter's three dreams first, Acts 10.)

Dream One: A flat, white sheet, with four ropes tied to the corners, descended from over my bed. On the sheet were three books: an Old Testament, the New Testament, and a Quran. "I read only the New Testament," I called out. "The other two are uninspired."

The Voice spoke: "Do not call uninspired what the **'Great I Am'** has caused to be written. These three books record mankind's efforts to know God; as well as God's attempt to be known by humankind."

Dream Two: Again the sheet descended. This time it contained miniature models of three buildings: a Jewish temple and a church and a mosque. The Voice spoke again, "All three are houses of God, but God is not housed in any one of them, nor all three of them, nor in any earthly facility."

Dream Three: This time the sheet contained a kneeling mat and a rosary and a prayer cap. And this time I spoke first: "Wrong. I am a protestant. I do not need props to pray."

The Voice: "Right. Prayer is just speaking with the Creator-Creating God, with an attitude of gratitude, a sincere desire to become all one was meant to be, and a willingness to be co-creative with God, as one is lead. And remember," the Voice concluded, "all creatures are important to the Creator. Do not call any person, or any denomination common. Respect all things, for everything is unique and beautiful in it's own way."

My dream concluded with these words of Peter: "I now realize how true it is that God does not show favoritism but accepts men (and women) from every nation who fear him and do what is right." (Acts 10:34) The New International version.

An Evangelical Christian
and A Liberal Christian
Talk about their Jesus

Evangelical Christian: "I believe the Holy Bible is the inspired Word of God and I believe every word in it. The Bible is the infallible Word of God. The Bible is inerrant."

Liberal Christian: "If you believe that then you really do not know what is in the Bible. The men who wrote the bible thought the earth was flat and had four corners. Thinking that the sun rose in the east and set in the west, they recorded that God stopped the sun from circling the earth to permit more day light so Joshua's troops could kill more of their enemies. The Bible has two different creation stories in the first three chapters of Genesis that repudiate each other; and neither of the two answers the question, 'Where did Cain and Abel find their wives?'"

E. C. : "I believe God created Adam and Eve in six days as the Bible states. Do you believe we came from monkeys?"

L. C. : "Have you even read Darwin's theory of evolution (survival of the fittest)? Listen, all you have to do is follow the development process of the human embryo from conception to birth. At one stage the potential baby has GILLS like a fish, and at another stage it has a LONG TAIL, as you say, like a monkey. It seems to me the process is self explanatory."

E. C. : "Let me ask you a personal question. Do you believe that Jesus died for your sins and that by His precious blood we are saved?

L. C. : "Absolutely not. Jesus was killed because he spoke out against the Roman way of treating their captives. He was a trouble maker and a disturber of the Roman system of government. Jesus taught of another Empire (kingdom) rather than the Roman Empire; and was crucified as the King of the Jews, the title which was nailed above his head on his cross. **Jesus as a human sacrifice was Paul's idea.** Remember, Paul was high up in the Jewish bureaucracy, living before the temple in Jerusalem was destroyed in 70 A.D. The Jews offered animal sacrifices daily and it was Paul's transference of this sacrificial system to the death of Jesus that created this substitutionary atonement doctrine. The Jews have long since ceased to offer sacrifices and think the custom to have been a primitive form of worship. I think it is time you conservative Christians do the same. Now, if I may, let me ask you a personal question. Why do you think God created us in the first place?"

E.C. : "That's easy. To be 'saved' and then to live with God in heaven forever. Why do you think he created you?"

L. C. : "I was hoping you would reciprocate that question. I believe God created us to enjoy the flowers, and music (from the song of the birds to symphonies), and family life, and pleasant conversational exchanges with friends, and to learn how to respond to God's love by loving our neighbors and to experience the satisfaction of helping those who are in need of food, or clothing, or attention or financial assistance. Not saved to go to heaven; but 'saved' to serve and to share. It is the most important lesson a child can learn in grammar school, to share, and it is the most important idea we can learn to fulfill before we die. If there is a heaven, everyone who enters should have a recommendation from the poor."

E.C. : "That is pure liberal, humanistic garbage. Why, it's not even a good social gospel. You have no Christology, no hope of salvation. I'll bet you don't even believe in the resurrection, yet you call yourself a Christian."

L.C. : "Oh, but I do. But let me elaborate. I believe in a resurrection, not a resuscitation. When the spirit of Jesus, his teachings, his attitude toward the poor, his compassion for the needy, when his spirit is understood and personified, then the resurrection has occurred. Jesus lives to the degree that he is revealed by his disciples, then and now. I believe human beings are spiritual beings dwelling within physical bodies. When God, as the Spirit in Christ, becomes known by our spirit, then resurrection has occurred."

E.C. : "I believe that 'God so loved the world that he gave his only begotten son, and that whosoever believes in Him shall have everlasting life.' Do you?"

L.C. : "Yeah, your love and concern for God's world overwhelms me. But let me paraphrase. I believe that God so loves the world that he gave Jesus the responsibility to teach and exemplify the love principle expressed in love for neighbor and self. Indeed, Jesus' major contribution was not dying for us, bur living a life of love for us to demonstrate how God wishes us to live."

E.C. : "I believe 'God was in Christ reconciling the world unto Himself.'"

L.C. : "So do I. I am just taking it a step or two further and trying to explain to a modern world what these 2,000 year old phrases mean."

E.C. : "I'm tired of listening to your liberal, socialistic humanism. I believe that Jesus Christ is the only Son of God who died for me and offers me eternal life. I believe that Jesus is the only way to heaven, and if you do not believe that, then you can go to hell! This discussion is over."

But it should not be...

Note from the dreamer-author: Of course, being a true Methodist preacher, I would sooner or later dream of chatting with the founder of Methodism, **Dr. John Wesley**. Here is the scene setting up this dream:

Four of us, Samuel Wesley, Jr., John Wesley, Charles Wesley and I were seated at an oversized rectangular table.

Three of us, Samuel, John and Charles, the Wesley brothers, wore 18th century clerical collars.

Two of us, John and Charles, had journals before them recording the meeting.

One of us, myself in particular, was quite nervous. I had been a Methodist all of my life; so I knew the opportunity this dream would afford.

I started the discussion: "Gentlemen, before you tell me about the beginnings of Methodism or whatever; I want to tell the three of you how much your father's poem of the 'Life of Christ' means to me. I thoroughly enjoy reading his poetic translation of the entire gospel, and I read from it often."

I continued, "I have memorized the prayer he places on the lips of the Publican, and I also pray it often:
'O Thou, whose eyes the souls of men survey,
And viewest their actions in the light of day,
Thou knowest the crimes I tremblingly confess,
And seest the passions which my soul possess,
For all my crimes, Thy mercy I implore,
And ask Thy grace that I may sin no more'."

Charles, the youngest brother, responds first: "As John has given our mother credit for teaching him his organizational skills, so I am indebted to our dad for showing me how to rhyme a verse. You may also know that dad composed not a few hymns. Most of them were destroyed by the fire of the Epworth rectory where brother John almost lost his life."

Samuel, the oldest brother spoke next: "Yes, after that fire; the next day I picked through the ashes and found a few relics of his papers. Among them I remember finding this hymn which I have prized over the years:

> *'Behold the Savior of mankind*
> *Nailed to that shameful tree;*
> *How vast the love that Him inclined*
> *To bleed and die for thee!*
>
> *'Tis done! The precious ransom's paid!*
> *"Receive my soul," He cries.*
> *See where He bows His sacred head;*
> *He bows His head and dies!*
>
> *But soon He'll break death's envious chain*
> *And in full glory shine,*
> *O Lamb of God, was ever pain,*
> *Was ever love like Thine?'"*

Me: "Charles, while we are speaking of hymns, may I say that your Christmas hymn, 'Hark, the Herald Angels Sing' and your Easter hymn, 'Christ the Lord is Risen Today' are two of my all time favorites. I wonder, would it be fair to ask you which is your favorite of the hundreds that you have composed?"

Charles: "There are three: 'O Love Divine,' 'A Charge To Keep I Have,' and 'Love Divine, All Loves Excelling'."

John: "If I may interject an opinion, I prefer brother Charles' hymn 'Jesus Lord, We Look To Thee'. If we could but sing it often and abide by it's message daily, we would have a world filled with warm hearts and kindly deeds."

Me: "I am sure you know I want to pick up on your phrase 'warm hearts'; and specifically your 'heart warming experience' at the Moravian prayer meeting. But first, let's talk a little about some of your 'heart breaking' experiences with women. One in particular interests me even more than your relationship with Sophy Hopkey in America. Charles, has John ever forgiven you for intervening in his intended marriage to Grace Murry?"

Charles: "In retrospect, I acted quite badly. I felt strongly that John should not marry at that time; but I should have remained neutral and trusted John's integrity."

John: "I now believe that brother Charles did what he felt to be the proper action for the sake of the movement. Also, I waited too late to make my intentions known. The unhappy marriages of our sisters, and finding someone as wonderful as our mother, caused me to prolong my decision about marriage. Besides, at that time my daily routine was too full to permit it. Charles was right. To marry at that time would have been a mistake."

Me: "John, you recorded in your journal about your assurance of salvation which you received that night when you reluctantly attended a Bible study. Would you please elaborate?"

John: "During a sea voyage, we encountered a horrific storm. Our ship almost sank; and I am ashamed to admit it, but my hope for life did sink. I was terribly frightened. I realized that I was not ready to die! I who had gone to America to save the Indians, was not saved myself. Later, at that Moravian prayer meeting, I experienced the personalization of salvation. I knew, academically, that Christ was the Savior of the world; but I did not know until then that He was my Savior. This private, spiritually satisfying relationship in Christ was based on God's grace and mercy; and not on educational achievement, or credits for mission field sufferings, nor none of the rewards of good works... just faith in God's love and mercy and grace as these elements culminate in the life and teachings, death and resurrection of Jesus Christ."

John continued talking about his 'heart warming' experience: "I am indebted to Martin Luther for his elaboration on St. Paul's letter to Rome; and I refer all your dream readers to seek out that personal relationship presented so profoundly in that Pauline epistle. Indeed, 'the just shall live (and die) by faith'."

Me: "Dr. Wesley, am I correct in thinking that you did not wish to start a new denomination? You wanted to remain in the Anglican Church of England, but they closed their doors to you when you started preaching this 'personal salvation'?"

John: "That is absolutely correct. Therefore, with the help of George Whitfield, we took to the streets to preach the gospel. Similar to the method your present day Salvation Army does, but without the drums and trumpet and begging pots." The brothers laughed.

Me: "Samuel," I recognized the oldest brother again, "I feel I am beginning to awaken. Do you have a final word for those who may read my book?"

Samuel: "Certainly, just relax and **accept God's will for His children to live in harmony as brothers and sisters. Respect differences of opinion; and seek** to do the loving thing in **every possible relationship, God being** your helper. I think brother John said it well when he wrote:

'Do all the good you can...

By all the means you can,

In all the ways you can,

In all the places you can,

At all the times you can,

To all the people you can,

As long as ever you can.' "

Post-test on Denominations
(An Open Book True or False Test)

1. _____ Paul asked the question: "Is God the God of the Jews only?" Then he answers: "Yes!"

2. _____ Pope John Paul, II said that both rich and poor nations and people of all faiths should unite to end poverty and all forms of social discrimination; and that Roman Catholics must lead the way.

3. _____ Andrew introduced his brother, Simon Peter, to Jesus whom he later nick-named as Peter, the "Rock".

4. _____ Martin Luther respected the Jewish people.

5. _____ Martin Luther is the founder of Methodism.

6. _____ John Wesley is indebted to Martin Luther for his elaboration on St. Paul's letter to the Romans.

7. _____ According to John 17:21, Jesus prayed that we all may become healthy individuals.

8. _____ The content of a jar is not as important as the label on the outside of the jar. Of course, the goal is congruency.

9. _____ The Bible contains two different creation stories in the first three chapters of Genesis that repudiate each other.

10. _____ The dreamer-author feels that Christians disagree on some issues and that they should not.

CHRISTIANITY

AND

HUMANISM

Happy Human

Some Excerpts From Humanists

"An unexamined life is not worth living." Socrates

"How wonderful the world might be if we gave to each other all the love we claim to give to God. Such a world can be ours, sisters and brothers. Let us work together to achieve it."
John J. Dunphy

""The world is my country, all mankind are my brethren, and to do good is my religion." Thomas Paine

"My religiosity consists in a humble admiration of the infinitely superior Spirit that reveals itself in the little that we, with our weak and transitory understanding, can comprehend of reality. Morality is of the highest importance; but for us, not for God." Albert Einstein

"The good life is one inspired by love and guided by knowledge." Bertrand Russell

"I can very well do without God both in my life and in my painting, but I cannot, suffering as I am, do without something which is greater than I am." Vincent Van Gogh

"In the faces of men and women I see God." Walt Whitman

The First Humanists

Socrates, Plato and Aristotle

Realizing that I was in the presence of three mental giants, I thought to myself, "Boy, this is really going to be a one sided dream." Nonetheless, as stupid as I felt, it was just a dream, so I began right away with questions. I did remember from my college philosophy class that dialogue was the Socratic method.

Me: "Is it true that you never wrote anything, Socrates?"

Socrates: "Only on the hearts of my students. My method was to sting students into awareness like a gadfly; and then to serve as midwife for their own mental travails."

Plato: "He asked insightful questions that enabled us (his students) to discover and decide for ourselves."

Aristotle: "My mentor, Plato, wrote of many dialogues he remembered his teacher, Socrates, having conducted. Therefore, as Socrates has spoken, his words were imprinted in the minds of Plato and Xenophon, who have recorded them for history and for philosophy."

Me: "Let me ask you about that Plato. Did you create words and ideas for Socrates in your writings or are your writings based on actual recollections?"

Plato: "Actually, both. If Socrates did not say those things, I knew him well enough to know that he should have." Plato glanced at his teacher. Their eyes met; and both smiled, as

Socrates nodded agreement.

Me: "Let me see if I understand correctly. You went about Athens questioning people, provoking discussions chiefly on ethical problems, inducing people to think? Will one of you illustrate that method for me?"

Aristotle: "Have you read Plato's recording of Socrates' dialogue with Enthyphro?"

Me: "Wait a minute; let me think."

All three philosophers broke into laughter. They seemed to have made their point to each other if not to me. Maybe you readers will catch it. Ignoring their laughter, I responded. I wanted them to know I was not completely ignorant: "Isn't that the one where Socrates cites the man who is testifying against his father for killing a murderer by leaving him cuffed and lying in a ditch to freeze to death as they waited for the police?"

Plato: "Good, now stay with that thought. Keep thinking, or rather start thinking. Did Socrates ever tell the informer that he may be wrong?"

Me: "No, he just kept questioning him until he decided for himself to leave the court, uncertain, but thinking. I get it. Thank you. Now I have a question for Aristotle. How did you feel about your famous pupil Alexander, the Great?"

Aristotle: "My objective as his tutor was to give him information and to teach him how to think. I am satisfied I did my job. It just took Alexander a long time to realize that it is futile to conquer a nation without conquering the hearts of the people of that nation."

Me: "Listen fellows, I will probably be waking soon. Please give me something I can remember from each of you."

Socrates: "An unexamined life is not worth living."

Plato: **"A. Man is continually evolving.**
       B. Evolution requires a first cause.
       C. Therefore, by whatever the name,
          The Prime Mover (Demiurge) still moves."

Aristotle: "Have you read Plato's 'Apology'?"

When I looked puzzled at Aristotle's question, they all three burst into laughter again; and I again, did not understand the joke. I awakened wondering what was so damned funny; but quickly took pen in hand and recorded this dream as I remembered it.

I also remembered the words of my old Army sergeant to us foot soldiers, "Ours is not to reason why; ours is to do or die!" "Not everyone is destined to be a great thinker," I thought as I turned over and went back to sleep.

A Poem and A Prayer of Michelangelo

I have had the pleasure of scrutinizing the 'Pieta' - that marble statue of Jesus' young mother holding his lifeless body just after the crucifixion - on loan from St. Peter's in Rome. Another of my favorite Michelangelo masterpieces is the fresco, 'the Creation of Adam' as it appears in the ceiling of the Sistine Chapel. The almost touching of the fingers is a fascinating concept to me. The sensitive observer can almost feel the spark of life that jumps from God's finger into man's body. The touch of God...the spirit of man! Needless to say, I was thrilled to be visited in a dream by this great artist.

I recognized him right off...his crooked nose, caused by a fight when he was a youth, had marked him for life; and the strange manner in which he held his head. In fact, as he first appeared in my dream, he was holding a letter above his eyes as he read it. He had to hold the letter above his head in order to read it because of working with his head back and arms raised above his head almost daily for a period of about four years. Incidentally, that ceiling was sixty five feet up!

I began, "I am delighted to meet you sir. May I ask you a few questions about your life's work?"

"No thank you," he quickly and coldly responded. "I am not interested in an interview and I am too busy for idle chat."

"It will not take long, I promise," I assured him.

"Very well then, a couple of questions," he agreed, "and be quick about it. My paint is calcifying as you detain me."

What one or two questions would I, or should I, ask this masterful architect, artist, fresco painter, sculptor and poet… not of his famous frescoes, nor of his 'Moses' statue, not even how he took someone else's unfinished statue of a giant and chiseled the magnificent 'David'. Perhaps of his rivalry with Raphael and/or Leonardo da Vinci?

Michelangelo: "Please hurry."

Me: "Sir, your nudes have such realistic muscle form that seem to be quivering with life. How? How did you make your statues so life like? Is it just a God given talent?"

Michelangelo: "By no means. The prior of Santo Spirito gave me a den in an Augustinian hospital for the poor where I spent long hours dissecting cadavers and thereby learned about the networks of muscles and tendons. And it was by no means an easy discipline. This ghoulish course of study cast a pall over my spirit and affected my digestion indefinitely. But this is where I learned about the human anatomy."

"Jesus," I uttered out loud, "I am shocked."

Michelangelo continued: "Then too, I had gifted teachers. **My work became a spiritual fulfillment for me, my only comfort, my work was my daily prayer.** I never married, had few friends, worked for days with little food, did not care how I dressed. Once I remember that for months on end, day and night, I wore cheap boots over my bare feet; when I finally got around to taking them off, bits of the soles of my feet came off with them."

Me: "Jesus," I heard myself say again. Then I asked, "About your familiarity with the human body, is it true that you painted a subliminal picture of the human brain surrounding the image of God in the **'creation of Adam'** ceiling fresco?"

Michelangelo: "Well, whether intended or not, it is there to be seen by the observant viewer."

Me: "I also heard a rumor from one of the tour guides at the Sistine Chapel that you sneaked into the chapel the night before the grand opening and painted a caricature of the then assistant to the pope, giving him donkey ears and painting a serpent around his waist, gnawing on his scrotum."

Michelangelo: "Yes, the assistant to the pontiff kept bothering me as I tried to finish my tedious work. And as you may know I am a perfectionist. And perfection takes time and patience and erasures and re-painting. He hurried me daily and reviled me publicly, even before my work was finished. But after the public recognized the caricature of Birgio da Cesena, no one bothered me anymore in my future work."

Me: "I can readily see why no one did; but you surely do have some nerve. Yet as hard as you worked, you left many unfinished projects. You must have had too many things going at one time."

Michelangelo: "Yes, and like you, everyone demanded too much of my time. So if you will excuse me, I must get back to my work."

Me: "As you wish." Quite frankly, my feelings were hurt by

his abrupt and nonfriendly mannerism. However, I recalled from biographies of him, that he treated popes and dignitaries the same way. **Perhaps he feels his statues and frescoes speak for him.**

As he was leaving, Michelangelo handed me a piece of paper that had one of his sketches on one side; and on the other side, two pieces of his poetry. After reading them, my appreciation of his struggles increased. I have attached his provocative poems which to me, reveal his Neo-Platonism philosophy/theology of a soul trapped in a physical body being joyfully freed at one's death. **Michelangelo's poems:**

> "If true (and it is) that with body's final breath
> the soul, cut loose from flesh (which it only bore
> because heaven imposed that chore),
> breaks free, it feels only then supreme delight,
> becoming divine in death
> as sure as we're born, down here, with death in sight.
> No sin is this; we're right
> to change funeral woe to mirth
> When we stand about to mourn the newly dead,
> For the soul, escaping earth
> and the frail remains, then, there, on the deathbed;
> finds perfect peace instead.
> Such their true friends desire, in equal measure
> as **pleasure in God transcends all earthly treasure.**"

> "Day in, day out, from childhood long ago,
> You were my one sole help and guide, O Lord,
> That's why my soul looks confidently toward
> Your double comfort in my double woe."

"Gentlemen," I addressed George Washington, Thomas Jefferson and John Adams. "What is the format of this dream?" I asked.

"Well, it is your dream," replied the First General. "Why not ask your questions and we will answer accordingly."

"Very well then," I agree. "General, let me begin with you. Did you in fact cut down that cherry tree?"

"If I may interject," John Adams interrupted in a very course manner, "That illustration became popular because George Washington was a man of his word. If he gave you his word, you would know that he would not change his position, even if it became an unpopular issue."

For some reason, I was still in a light mood. I again addressed the general, "And did you stand up in that boat as you crossed the Delaware?" Again I smiled.

And again John Adams interrupted, "Of course not. Get serious dreamer. Valley Forge was not a laughing matter. That now famous painting emphasizes General Washington's brilliant surprise attack when the British were sitting back waiting for our revolutionists to freeze and die of hunger."

With the mention of that horrible Valley Forge winter, my mood sobered. But before I could ask a serious question, General Washington spoke up, "Before you ask your next question, let me assure you that I was too frugal to throw a dollar across some river."

We all laughed, and then I went for it. Changing my interests to Thomas Jefferson, "Mr. Jefferson, you wrote that all men are created equally; and yet you owned over two hundred slaves. Please clarify that inconsistency"

Once more John Adams interrupted, "Listen carefully dreamer, times were different back then.. Over one fifth of the population were slaves...owned human beings. And before you go there, he owned Sally Hemings also. She was his local property, to do with, or to do without, as he pleased."

"Mr. Jefferson?" I again ignored Mr. Adams' response as I looked directly into Jefferson's eyes.

As he did when the British got close to his Monticello, Mr. Jefferson walked away. Again John Adams came to Jefferson's defense, "Dreamer, it was the man that you are determined to discredit that doubled America's land area by purchasing from Napoleon the entire Louisiana territory. He also got the separation of church and state amendment passed into Virginia laws. Not to mention he financed the Lewis and Clark expedition."

Not to be put off by his accomplishments, I called out to Mr. Jefferson once more, "Sir, did you not state publicly that a child raised every two years by a slave woman is of more profit than the crop of the best laboring man? And even more to the point, did you not carry on an affair with a slave mistress; fathering as many as six children by her?"

Slowly Thomas Jefferson walked back among us and finally spoke, "You refer to my relationship with Miss Sally Hemings. She was my wife's half-sister. And though color is not the issue you raise, she was only one-quarter black. She accompanied me when I was minister to France; and I spent as much money on her dresses as I did for my daughters."

Almost as if he wanted to confess all, he continued, "Back at Monticello, Sally lived in the main house and was in charge of my 'chamber and wardrobe'. She was indeed the lady of the entire house. And one further point you might find of interest, dreamer, Sally was considered free while in France, but she chose to return to America with me."

I chose to remain quiet this time; as I felt he needed space to gather his closure. He had revealed much; but still had not said either yes or no.

After a brief pause, he continued, "Of course you are right dreamer, **it is in our life and not in our words that our religion must be read.** However, none of us is perfect; and were we to love none who had imperfections, this world would be a desert for our love."

"Your point is well made," I mellowed. (I chose not to confront him with the 1998 DNA testing results that strongly suggested his paternity) Instead, I said, "I just think the truth should out and that truth will speak for itself. But now, before I wake, what advice do you three fore-fathers have for us as Americans in the twenty first century? Please answer chronologically as you served this country as president."

Washington confessed: "After what you put president Jefferson through, I felt sure you would attack me on my reputation of sleeping around. After all, 'George Washington slept here!' used to be a standard joke."

We all laughed, then I requested, "Will you make a comment about **humanism** and **religion**?" George Washington: "Reason and experience both forbid us to expect that national morality can prevail in exclusion of religious principles. Our country needs people who value both education and religion, not either/or."

"Thank you sir, well said," I complimented him. Then I turned to John Adams. It pleased me that he had waited his turn. "President Adams, will you say a word about your **religious beliefs**?"

Adams: "I believe in God, his wisdom and benevolence; and I cannot conceive that such a Being could make such a species as the human merely to live and die on this earth. I watch a worm wrap itself in a cocoon, go to sleep and wake as a beautiful butterfly. I pick up a tiny acorn and hold the potential of a towering oak tree in my hand. A bird births from an egg and sings and soars; from a bulb, a fragrant flower, and from my dead body, a resurrected soul. That's a few of the reasons I believe in a future state." Then Adams turned and looked to Jefferson for his forthcoming statement. And for the first time, I had a good feeling toward President Adams.

"And President Jefferson, since you are a Deist and more influenced by the reason-centered Enlightenment, I would be interested in your view of **denominational unity**." I requested.

Jefferson: "I believe there is not a Quaker or a Baptist, a Presbyterian or an Episcopalian, a Catholic or a Protestant in heaven; that, on entering that gate, we leave these badges of schism behind, and find ourselves united in those principles only in which God has united us all. Let us not be uneasy then, about the different roads we may pursue to find the **One God.**"

After all three had contributed, they turned their backs to me and slowly walked out of my dream... fading into a fog like background. As they disappeared, I heard John Adams once more interrupt the silence by asking Thomas Jefferson, "Thomas, would you go back to your cradle and live over again your seventy years?"

Thomas Jefferson's response, "I say yes. I think with you it is a good world on the whole; that it has been framed on a principle of benevolence, and more pleasure than pain delt out to us. I steer my bark with hope in the head, leaving fear astern."

"Hear, hear," said the first general and first president. The other great statesman nodded, as they disappeared into the fog of history again. My feeling as I recorded this dream, "I wished I had asked better questions of such a momentous occasion."

The Doctor

Eight nights after I had read Ben Franklin's autobiography, he appeared in one of my dreams.

He wore bi-focals, of course, and leaning against his leg was that famous crab-tree walking stick with it's gold head in the form of a cap of liberty (which Ben Franklin willed to "my friend, and the friend of mankind, George Washington").

There was a silk kite with a key still attached by a ribbon hanging on his wall; along with a framed copy of the Declaration of Independence.

What surprised me was he was playing drinking glasses. I called out as he continued to play, "Dr. Franklin, I knew you invented bi-focals for reading glasses, but I did not know that you played glasses also."

My play-on-words joke drew a serious response: "O yes, this is an armonica. It is based on sounds that I get when I rub my wet fingers around the rims of these glasses which I have filled with varying amounts of water. As you can see, I have made these special glasses and placed them on a horizontal spinning wheel."

"Sir, if you will but stop playing for a few minutes, there are some questions I would like to ask you," I requested.

He looked at me over both sets of his glasses and then stopped playing. "How can I help you, my boy?" he volunteered. I smiled. I was sixty years old; but old Ben was in his eighties.

"Well, first I want to know about that kite," I began. "You didn't say much about it in your autobiography."

"What's to say?" he replied. "My lightening rods speak for themselves. When I coined the phrases 'positive and negative' or 'plus and minus' for 'vitrecous and resinour' electricity, that was a real break through," he laughed. "And that day I almost electrocuted myself, I felt like the man who, trying to steal powder, made a hole in the cast with a hot iron. Now the electrical battery, that was a good discovery/invention. But if you want to know more about the kite experiment, read the Joe Priestly account. I gave him the precise details," Dr. Franklin concluded.

"Is it true, sir, that you did not profit from the sell of your lightening rods?" I doubtingly asked.

"Yes, that is true," he admitted. "Some say I found electricity a curiosity and left it a science. The more poetic have written how I plucked fire from the sky. I choose to say I was just lucky with my guesses; and I am content to see in your world today what wonderful things have been developed by using electricity."

"Well said," I praised him. "Now will you give me a few of your favorite sayings from your Poor Richard's Almanac."

"All right," he complied:

1. "Content makes poor men rich;
   discontent makes rich men poor."

2. "Fish and visitors stink after three days."

3. "He that would live in peace and at ease,
   must not speak all he knows, nor judge all he sees."

4. "And here is my favorite: 'Little strokes fell great oaks'."

"Thank you," I expressed. "Now, concerning religion, I remember that you wrote in one of you Almanacs: 'You will be careful if you are wise, how you touch men's religion or credit or eyes'. But I want to ask you about that now famous letter you wrote to the then president of Yale University. In it you affirmed your belief in **one God** as Creator of the universe. You also stated in that letter that the most acceptable service we render Him is doing good to His other children. As to Jesus of Nazareth you wrote that his system of morals and his religion is the best this old world has ever seen and is likely to see; but in my opinion, you hedged as to the divinity of Christ. Would you like to clarify that position now?"

"No," the doctor responded. "Let those statements about religion that I made in that correspondence to Dr. Ezra Stiles stand. I would only reiterate: 'I left this world in peace with all religions. **Would to God all religions could live in peace.**' I recall one glorious 4th of July back in 1787 where I watched from my window because I was too sick to attend the parade, when for the first time in its history, Philadelphia saw the clergy of almost all the different Christian denominations, with the rabbi of the Jews, walking arm in arm."

"And has your self-written epitaph been fulfilled?" I concluded.

"Indeed it has," he affirmed with a beautiful smile. Then he went back to playing his partially filled glasses; and I returned to my dream journaling, thankful that I too, expect to be Revised by the Author.

The self-written epitaph of Benjamin Franklin:

"The body of Benjamin Franklin, printer.

Like the covering of an old book…

Its contents torn out,

And stript of its lettering and gilding,

Lies here, food for worms;

But the work shall not be lost,

It will (as he believed) appear once more…

In a new and more beautiful edition,

Corrected and amended

By the Author."

On Interpreting Dreams

In this dream I meet two of the world's greatest dreamers; or at least, two of the world's greatest interpreters of dreams: Sigmund Freud and Carl Gustav Jung.

I opened my eyes (in my dream) and found myself lying on a couch in a strange room. I turned my head slightly to the right and immediately recognized Sigmund Freud sitting there, notepad in hand, with a lit cigar in his mouth.

"Sir, that cigar has to go. I simply cannot breathe around the smoke of it." I dared to tell him.

"It is a pity that the man who introduced us to Phallic symbols cannot recognize his own," a male voice from my left suggested. I turned my head his way and immediately recognized Carl Jung.

"You two are still at it I see," I commented. Having read all of their published letters, I knew of their differences concerning psychoanalysis, a treatment using free association.

So, I knew that Freud would rebuttal. I turned my head back to the right to hear his next comment. He said, quite bluntly, "Let me give you a brief word association test, Carl. What is the first word that comes to mind when you hear the word 'jackass'?"

I laughed to myself and turned again to catch Jung's response (the genius of Dr. Freud's juxtaposition was, as you may know, Dr. Jung invented the word association test).

"Let's see," Dr. Jung pondered, "the first word that comes to my mind when I hear the word 'jackass' is 'Freud'.

This time I laughed out loud. Jung was equal to the dialogue. "Come on, guys," I begged, "Give me a break here. This dream is a chance of a life time for me to learn some things about dreams. Let me ask you this: 'Granted, in your time, sex was a repressed issue; but today sex is openly discussed. If you lived today, wouldn't you change your major thesis of repressed sexual desires stimulating the unconscious?"

"Not at all," Dr. Freud responded. "Sex and death, the fear of them, the mystery around them and their influence on most everyone are still the major stress inducers."

Dr. Freud continued: "The importance of how other people view us would be my differing approach today; but still the stress centers around how others view us as lovers who satisfy and as livers who are successful before death."

"Livers?" Dr. Jung interrupted. "Might that be a Freudian slip old boy? Care to free associate that one."

Before Freud could rebuttal, I jumped in: "All right Jung, here's a question for you. You have analyzed over 80,000 dreams. From that research, are some of our dreams stimulated by your collective unconscious; therefore urging us to become individuated into a wholesome Self, spelled with a capital 's' of course?"

Jung replied, seemingly quite pleased with my familiarity

with the thesis of his work, "Yes, yes indeed. You have got it right. Now Freud never wanted me to get involved with religions and the occults, but all of my research into the unconscious reveals a God-force who can be known, not only believed in; and who calls us to become a mature and completed Self; through the process of individuation, of course."

"Bull shit," said Freud. "You both sound like spiritual neurotics. Your desire for God is simply a wish fulfillment for the father figure you never had."

Dr. Jung started to rebuttal when I raised my hand and said, "Let me take this one. If I might be so bold, that is simply your own defense mechanism 'projection' Dr. Freud; for I have read of your own Oedipal complex (love of mother; jealousy of father)."

"Point well made," added Dr. Jung. Then Freud asked Jung, point blank, "Carl, do you really believe some dreams are divinely inspired, that there is a God who speaks this way?"

"Siggie, like I said in my summation of my Terry Lectures: 'Religious experience is absolute… and no matter what the world thinks about religious experience, the one who has it possesses a great treasury, a thing that has become, for him a source of light, meaning and beauty; and has given a new splendor to the world and to mankind. He has faith and peace and further, if such experience helps to make your life healthier, more beautiful, more complete and more satisfying to yourself and to those you love, you may safely say, '**This was the grace of God**'."

4 Believers vs.

1 Humanist

Four believers converge on a humanist, each wishing to convert the non-believer to their way of thinking. In alphabetical order, they try to impress the humanist.

Buddhist: "A lotus to you, a Buddhist to be. I offer you enlightenment. First, forget suffering. It is universal. The secret lies in the middle way of no desire. Want not, and you will not be disappointed. Just be content in every situation. Everything is relative. Enjoy the moment. Just be."

Christian: "We Christians are a diverse group. Some of us still are known as 'vampire' Christians - 'Washed in the Blood of the Lamb', while others are so liberal that 'love' is the only absolute. Forgiveness of sins and 'new life' in Christ are our biggies. Some of us still believe that our Jesus is the only way to 'pie-in-the-sky-bye-and-bye', but others see God revealing Himself in other religions. We invite you to join us. Our invitation: "God loves you; and we love you!" Check us out.

Jew: "We Jews are God's favorite people. We are known as the 'frozen chosen' because we are the oldest religion and we have worked most of the kinks out of our beliefs. For us, it is quite simple. Obey the ten commandments and love God with your whole heart and your neighbor as yourself. We worship on Friday nights, so we have Sunday as a free day."

Muslim: "Listen up. The answer to your religious quest is submission. We submit to Allah's will and follow the teachings of God as recited to Mohammed by the angel Gabriel and recorded verbatim in our holy book, the Quran. We stay God-centered by praying five times a day and by fasting during the month of Ramadan. We Muslim brothers take care of our orphans and widows. Join us and be secure."

Humanist: "I thank all four of you for trying to 'save' me, but I believe I'll keep my **eclectic view of religion**. You see, from the Jewish Old Testament I like Micah 6:8 'What does the Lord require of thee: to do justly, love mercifully, and walk humbly...' From Jesus, love and service. From the Buddha, living in the 'here and now', and from Mohammad, seeking to determine and submit to the will of Allah or Yahweh or Father God or whatever one chooses to call the **One Creative Force of all creation.**

The humanist concluded: "It seems to me you fellows need to concentrate on those things you have in common and respect each other's peculiarities more. However, you may feel free to call on me again whenever you are better coordinated. In the mean time, I will be watching your life styles to see if you live out your beliefs. How one acts impresses me more then what one thinks. Indeed, one's beliefs and one's actions should be in congruity."

A Noble Peace Prize Winner

This time, I dream traveled to a tiny village on the banks of the Mbashe River, 800 miles east of Cape Town and about 550 miles south of Johannesburg.

I stood before three huts...one used for cooking, one for sleeping, and one for storage. No furniture; only mats for sleeping. The inhabitants sat on the ground. They ate mostly maize (corn, which they called mealies), sorghum, beans and pumpkins.

The little boy's father was a chieftain. His mother was one of his father's four wives. He attended the Methodist mission school, then off to Wesleyan College; and finally to University College of Port Hare, which was for a young black South African, Oxford and Cambridge and Harvard and Yale all rolled into one.

However, he was expelled from Port Hare because he participated in a protest rally; and had to earn his law degree by correspondence. Nonetheless, in 1952, he became half of a law partnership...the first black law practice in Johannesburg.

But hold on, let me let you hear it as I did in the dream that followed my research of **Nelson Mandela**:

"I was born in Umtata, Transkei, on 18, July 1918. My father, chief Henry, was a polygamist with four wives. Neither he nor my mother ever went to school. I hold the degree of Bachelor of Arts from the University of South Africa, and am a qualified lawyer. My political interest was first aroused when I listened to elders of our tribe in my village as a youth. They spoke of the good old days before the arrival of the white man."

Mandela continues: "Because my people were treated so unfairly, I joined the African National Congress and became a freedom fighter."

Me: "And a terrorist!" I was surprised to hear myself interrupt. "I am very sorry sir," I apologized. "But I have never understood how a terrorist who advocated violence could ever be awarded the Nobel Peace Prize."

Mandela: "I do not deny that I planned sabotage. I did not plan it in a spirit of recklessness, nor because I have any love for violence. I planned it as a result of a calm and sober assessment of the political situation that had arisen after many years of tyranny, exploitation and oppression of my people by the whites."

Mandela explains: "Four forms of violence are possible. There is sabotage, there is guerrilla warfare, there is terrorism, and there is open revolution. We chose to adopt the first method and to test it fully before taking any other decision. In the light of our political background, the choice was a logical one. Sabotage did not involve loss of life and it offered the best hope for future race relations."

Me: "Well it got you over twenty five years in prison. I have been a prison chaplain and I know how devastating a few years of incarceration can be. Yet you have such a gentle personality.

How have you been able to overcome the bitterness?"

Mandela: "Perhaps if I was idle and did not have a job to do, I would be as bitter as others. But because I have been given a job to do, I have not had time to think about the cruel experiences I've had. I'm not unique though, others have every reason to be more bitter than I. There are countless people who went to jail and aren't bitter at all, because they can see that their sacrifices were not in vain, and the ideas for which we lived and sacrificed are about to come to fruition. And that removes the bitterness from their hearts."

Mandela continues: "During my lifetime I have dedicated my life to this struggle of the African people. I have fought against white domination, and I have fought against black domination. I have cherished the ideal of a democratic and free society in which **all persons live together in harmony with equal opportunities.** It is an ideal which I hope to live for, and to see realized. But if need be, it is an ideal for which I am prepared to die."

Me: "Sir, before this dream comes to an end, I want you to know that this dream interview will probably appear in my book about religion, and more specifically, a book about commonalities all religions share. Will you give me a quote concerning your opinion of religions?"

Nelson Mandela: "**Religion is one of the most important forces in the world. Whether you are a Christian, a Muslim, a Buddhist, a Jew, or a Hindu, religion is a great force, and it can help one have command of one's own morality, one's own behavior, and one's own attitude.**"

A CHRISTIAN HUMANIST
AND
A HEDONIST

In this dream, I am being interviewed by a hedonist:

Me: "You say 'Big Bang'; I say 'Big God'. And even if it was a 'Big Bang', God planned and caused it. I don't think creation just happened. I think creation has evolved. A telescoping into the vast universe, the earth's rotating around the sun, a mighty oak tree growing from a tiny acorn, a man or woman developing from an embryo, a brain that thinks, and reasons, and senses a Creator-creating God… all planned and designed by a Higher Being."

Hedonist: "Did you just say that you believe in evolution?"

Me: "Yes, a form of it anyway. I think evolution is probably how God did it. Not in six days as we today keep time. To me, time is a fourth dimension and not an important factor in the creation story. You see, I side with reason as far as our present scientific knowledge goes, but then I turn to faith. I believe in some things that have yet to be proven. I also believe in an indefinable spiritual world."

Hedonist: "That is pure foolishness. To go beyond facts is not realistic. I believe in only what I know to be scientifically proven. I hold to facts, not faith."

Me: "I understand. But how do you explain philosophical ideas like love, and truth, and beauty? These are concepts that cannot be placed under a microscope or 'felt' by a computer. **And if I may mix a little poetry with scientific knowledge:** to gaze upward into a starlit, summer sky, seeing hundreds of sparkling diamond-like stars which astronomers tell us are distant suns with no doubt planets circling them, causes my mind to feel the awesome, unfathomable thoughts of a Creator-creating God. Or to realize how our daughter came from my sperm planted lovingly inside my beautiful wife's womb, and after nine months of miraculous gestation, came forth and grew into the intelligent, amiable person she is today. Or via the process of homeostasis, the scientific name for the innate way the human body tends to heal itself, with the help of skilled physicians who cut into my heart and transplanted by-pass veins taken from my left leg. Or how I feel when my wife sits dutifully by my bedside until I resume consciousness and then kisses me gently after fifty years of friendship and child rearing. These are a few of the reasons I believe in a wonderful, loving God."

Hedonist: "Listen, there is no absolute truth. Everything is relative and can be explained from one's point of reference. And about love, if your God is a loving God, how can it send people to a hell?"

Me: "I do not think God sends anyone to a hell. I think people choose to go to hell of their own free wills. Just as I have chosen to go to heaven… if there is such a place."

Hedonist: "Then you do not believe in life after death?"

Me: "Yes, I believe my soul will continue to exist after it leaves my body, but I really have no idea as to what happens at that point. I believe, I trust, I hope, I pray… but I honestly do not know. But like a caterpillar that goes to sleep in it's cocoon and wakes as a beautiful butterfly, I look forward to such a transformation.

Hedonist: "How does one get to your heaven? What are the requirements for entrance?"

Me: "Well, I am a Christian, so that means Jesus is central to my religious beliefs. To me, Jesus was a lover - of all people, but primarily of the poor, the sickly, and the distraught. I believe Jesus received his strength by praying to a God, just as we can. I believe Jesus emptied himself of selfishness and greed and focused on finding pleasure in helping others. **Jesus personified love, and when we love, we experience God's greatest gift.** Not material things, but relationships - friends, neighbors, children, spouses - these are the important components of life."

I continued: "I also believe in a spiritual resurrection, but not a resuscitation. I believe, because of this resurrection, the Spirit of Jesus - his compassion, his empathy, his concern - still lives. I am aware of a God's presence in my life; and I experience his presence daily. I follow Jesus' advice: 'LOVE God with your whole being, and LOVE your neighbor and LOVE yourself.' I expect this blissful attitude to continue after my earthly death."

Hedonist: "You say you are aware of a God's presence, but do you honestly believe that a God is aware of everyone in the world and their unique situations?"

Me: "I look at that like a television station in reverse. Via television, a man in New York can be seen around the world. An unbelievable, and to me unexplainable invention. Surely, a very powerful and advanced Creator-creating God, who caused our entire galaxy, can somehow be aware of people's needs through out our little world."

Hedonist: "Okay, how about suffering? How can a good and all powerful God permit pain; or, in my opinion, only create an imperfect world, i.e., floods, hurricanes, cancer, etc.?"

Me: "Well, let's take the game of golf as an example. Without sand traps, water hazards, woods and tall grass - golf would be a very boring game. The traps make the game of golf more fun and challenging; and in like manner, pain and suffering encourage one to appreciate more 'no pain' and 'no suffering'. And in the same line of reasoning, let me mention freedom of choice, free to curse or create. I'll just say that without freedom of choice there could be no love. Think about it. We can bitch about our suffering, or we can choose to use and endure and try to cure our suffering. Actually, suffering is an opportunity!"

Hedonist: "Good point. Your God permits you to work it out for yourself. But does your God intervene?"

Me: "Occasionally, I guess just to let us know that He can and that He is unpredictable and that His power cannot be controlled by his creations. Usually though, when I present God with a problem, the answer is usually, 'I have given you a good brain, and the opportunity to attend schools, so use your brain and what you have learned and problem solve.'"

Hedonist: "In like manner, I have learned that you have to look after number one in this old world. You Christians hope for a pie-in-the-sky-bye-and-bye, but I believe in getting my piece of the pie in the here-and-now. I do not fear walking through the valley of shadows because I am the meanest and toughest son of a bitch in the valley."

Me: "We Christians have a saying. 'God loves you; and I love you'; but I must admit, you are making it hard. Nonetheless, I shall pray for you and I look forward to our next conversational exchange. I hope you stay well; and I trust that you will use your prosperity wisely. You asked me earlier what are the requirements to get to heaven. I believe that everyone who enters heaven must have a recommendation from the poor. It is not enough to believe in Jesus, one must LOVE as did Jesus."

Hedonist: "You know Reverend Starnes, I am surprised that you did not try to convince me that I am a sinner, that I am hell bent, and that I need your Jesus to be saved."

Me: "Actually, that's what I did. I just did not use the traditional fundamental terms. It's a new day for some Christians. Hope you will consider joining us."

The Dream Still Lives

Martin Luther King, Jr. is dead (murdered)...but his dream still inspires...still offers hope...still lives...

May his dream never be forgotten! May younger dreamers take up the non-violent demonstrations (when deemed necessary) and have the courage to walk the faith!

May the spirit of Rev. King, may the spirit of the King of kings, may the Holy Spirit, and the spirit of Christ sustain the dream and encourage new dreamers.

May we fulfill Martin's dream that one day **"all of God's children, black and white, Jews and Gentiles, Protestants and Catholics, will be able to join hands and sing..."**

May we have the courage to put hands and feet to the dream. May the Rev. Martin Luther King, Jr.'s dream become our dream. And may all our dreams end in peace! Amen.

Final Note from the Dreamer-Author:

"I sincerely pray that my writing has, to a degree, inspired my readers to live more fully, to love more deeply, and to laugh more often.

Whoever you are, wherever you may be, and whatever your religious beliefs, may the reading of this book have helped you to better understand other believers' search for our **One God.**

There are many paths that lead to the top of a mountain. Which ever path you choose, may you assist others who travel with you, and rejoice with those who climb a different path. The important thing is not so much the path one chooses, but that one climbs.

It seems to me that the closer we get to the top of our spiritual mountain, the closer we get to each other. Ideally, we can all come together at the top of our spiritual climb and, holding hands, enjoy the beautiful view of the world of our **One God.**

James A. Starnes

Post-test on Humanism

1. How did Socrates teach?

2. Michelangelo's statues and frescoes depict incredible and realistic muscle form. How did he perfect this God-given talent?

3. (A) According to Thomas Jefferson, how is one's religion read?

    (B) Why did Jefferson believe that there are no Baptist or Methodist in heaven?

4. What did Benjamin Franklin think of Jesus?

5. How did Carl Jung and Sigmund Freud differ about religion?

6. Which view of religion did the humanist choose when witnessed to by the Jew, the Muslim, the Christian and the Buddhist?

7. What are the beliefs of a Hedonist? Do you know one?

8. How can one who has planned sabotage be awarded the Nobel Peace Prize?

9. What is the major idea of Martin Luther King, Jr.'s dream?

10. What is the final hope that the dreamer-author of this book wishes for you, his readers?

The Cross at Beautiful
Lake Junaluska, N. C.

Questions about the content of this book may be addressed to:

Rev. James A. Starnes
111 Silver Circle
Lake Junaluska, N.C.
Zip Code: 28745